Stirring the Head, Heart, and Soul

In loving memory of my mother,
Hildur Kathryn Keturi,
my first-grade teacher,
my mentor, my friend

Stirring the Head, Heart, and Soul

Redefining Curriculum and Instruction

H. Lynn Erickson

CORWIN PRESS, INC.
A Sage Publications Company
Thousand Oaks, California

YORK COLLEGE
PENNSYLVANIA
Servire est vivere

For information address:

Corwin Press, Inc.
A Sage Publications Company
2455 Teller Road
Thousand Oaks, California 91320

SAGE Publications Ltd.
6 Bonhill Street
London EC2A 4PU
United Kingdom

SAGE Publications India Pvt. Ltd.
M-32 Market
Greater Kailash I
New Delhi 110 048 India

Printed in the United States of America

Library of Congress Cataloging-in-Publication Data

Erickson, H. Lynn.
    Stirring the head, heart, and soul: redefining curriculum and instruction /H. Lynn Erickson.
        p.   cm.
    Includes bibliographical references and index.
    ISBN 0-8039-6153-7 (alk. paper). — ISBN 0-8039-6154-5 (pbk. : alk. paper)
    1. Curriculum change—United States. 2. Curriculum-based assessment—United States. 3. Educational change—United States. 4. Educational tests and measurements—United States.   I. Title.
LB1570.E74   1995
375'.00973—dc20   94-31097

This book is printed on acid-free paper.

95 96 97 98 99 10 9 8 7 6 5 4 3 2

Corwin Press Production Editor: Diana E. Axelsen

Contents

Preface

Innovations are launched in schools like fireworks in July. Some explode with a bang, like the current "Whole Language" movement, and then whizzle back and forth trying to find their philosophical resting place. Some, like the "New Math" in the 1970s, shoot straight up and then nosedive, leaving a trail of fading light. Some give a little "pop," hoping for attention, and some, like the President's Goals and National Standards, implode with a sonic boom as we run for cover from the fallout.

As an educator over the past 26 years, I helped to detonate some of the most dazzling displays. Through these experiences, I gained a sense of when to tuck and when to toss from Innovation's door. Eager to aid learning, educators embrace innovation and fad with wholesale zealousness. We buy the program dogma with nary a question, disregarding the research that doesn't fit into the popular paradigm instead of asking, What is reasonable, what works, and what does not?

This book will discuss some of the reasonable and workable trends, show how they interrelate, and provide educators with a practical model for deciding whether to tuck or toss from the dizzying display of the day. The overriding trend throughout this book will be the Outcomes movement because it shifts the schooling focus from what students know to what they can do with what they know.

What a student can do is key to strong self-esteem, self-efficacy, and the love of learning.

The Outcomes movement, so popular today, defines Student Outcomes as what we want our students to know and be able to do by the time they graduate from high school. In districts across the United States, these outcomes deal with internal "process" skills, such as the ability to think or to communicate at high levels. Districts also develop one or two broad outcomes that call for content expertise and understanding. These content outcomes provide the anchor for aligning the district curriculum through concepts and topics of critical content.

National and state policymakers call for assessments of student performance, noting "benchmarks" of progress at various grade levels, to ensure that students are attaining the process and content abilities. Benchmarks are examples of developmental performance that have been identified for various grade levels or grade groupings. Benchmarks are the mileposts leading to the graduating Student Outcomes.

This trend to define Student Outcomes is welcome and long overdue. The demands of the 21st century require the development of highly sophisticated skills. But mandating an educational change of this magnitude without considering current structures in curriculum and instruction dooms the trend to sluggish ineptitude as ill-conceived plans are tossed on the problems like tattered blankets on burning coals.

This book will examine the current state of curriculum and instruction and propose a higher order curriculum model for achieving the graduation outcomes. The proposed model, based on critical, content-based concepts, will focus on the following premises:

- Thinking teachers inspire thinking students. We need Teacher Outcomes that parallel the Student Outcomes.
- Students and teachers who take personal responsibility for their work demonstrate thoughtful behavior, task interest, and increasing self-efficacy.
- Self-assessment is a powerful learning tool for both students and teachers.

- Curriculum that is relevant to issues surrounding the human condition and our world challenge the intellect and engage the spirit.

- *Concept-based curricula* are more effective than *topically based curricula*, for the world of today and tomorrow, because they take learning to a higher level as students analyze, synthesize, and generalize from facts to higher level knowledge.

- Concept-based, integrated curricula provide depth to learning and a focus on relevant issues, problems, and ideas.

As you read the following chapters, you will evaluate the elements and impediments of the change process in learning organizations and look at the factors of time, training, and funding. You will design a vision for learning that links desired student outcomes with sound schooling practice. You will learn new approaches to the development of subject area and integrated curricula and explore the changing character of student assessment. Finally, you will consider what it takes to stir the head, heart, and soul and form a vision of "loving to learn."

Students and teachers who love to learn create a positive tension and energy that ripples through a room with enthusiasm, curiosity, and creativity. It is my hope that you will leave this book with that same creative tension and energy—loving to learn and eager to stir the head, heart, and soul.

This book is written for teachers and curriculum leaders at all levels. The material is appropriate for all teachers who wish to understand the changing nature of curriculum and instruction. It is not a "make it and take it" book of cute ideas for Monday morning. It is an explanation of current trends in curriculum and instruction, set in the context of a changing world. It is a thoughtful "how to" of curriculum design and contains specific classroom examples.

A book is never written without past experiences and interactions. I would like to acknowledge the many friends and colleagues who have worked with me over the years, challenging my mind and stirring my head, heart, and soul. My deepest gratitude and thanks to all of the Coordinating Teachers in the Federal Way School District for their capable leadership in the design of quality curriculum; to

Sandy Huggins and Dr. Brenda McBrayer for their collaborative thoughts and leadership in the design of the Writing Indicators and the Language Arts Outcomes; to Pamela Sturgeon and Karen Moreau for their leadership in Concept-Based Science and the award-winning program written by more than 200 outstanding Federal Way teachers; to Steve Schuman for his assistance and collaboration on the performance assessment chapter; to all of the teachers in Federal Way who have given so generously of their time above and beyond the school day and year to design student-centered, concept-based curriculum; to Karen McKnight for her computer skill with the charts and figures in this book; and to Sherrelle Walker, Sally Lorenz-Reeves, and Leanna Isaacson for their valued reactions and quality advice on this manuscript.

About the Author

H. Lynn Erickson is a private consultant assisting schools and districts around the country with curriculum design. From 1987 to 1994, she was the Director of Curriculum for the Federal Way Public Schools in Federal Way, Washington. She was recently appointed by the governor's Commission on Student Learning to chair the Washington State Standards Committee for Social Studies. In her spare time she jumps on the Internet to communicate with teachers from her workshops on their progress with Integrated Curriculum units.

She was born and raised in Fairbanks, Alaska, the daughter of a pioneering gold miner and a first-grade teacher. She graduated from the University of Alaska in 1968 and taught first grade at North Pole, Alaska, before moving to Carlsbad, California. She taught first, second, fourth, and fifth grades, as well as combination classes, while in California. She also served for two years as a Reading Specialist. In 1976 she moved with her family to Missoula, Montana, and earned master's and doctorate degrees in Curriculum and Instruction and Advanced School Administration. She worked as the Curriculum Coordinator for Missoula's Public Schools before becoming an elementary principal for six years in Libby, Montana.

She has two grown children, Kelly and Kenneth; a son-in-law, Patrick Cameron; and a 2-year-old grandson, Trevor Cameron. They live in Washington State and she is able to visit them often. She enjoys watching Trevor develop, as he eagerly explores his world. His love of learning stirs her head, heart, and soul.

CHAPTER 1

Making Change in a Changing World

The State of Educational Change

Innovations and Restructuring

Everybody is doing it. Ask an elementary grade teacher in Anywhere, U.S.A., "What are the innovations in your school?" and the litany ensues: "Whole Language, cooperative learning, Integrated Curriculum, multiage, inclusion, portfolios, and so on." Secondary schools are joining many of the elementary grade movements and adding innovations of their own, from creative block scheduling to theme-based high schools.

The national impetus to restructure schools and improve education has brought us into the best and worst of times. The best of times:

- Engaging students in active and meaningful learning
- Looking beyond the memorization of low-level content **objectives** to the attainment of high-level graduation **outcomes** with a focus on the individual student
- Helping students develop greater self-efficacy and self-esteem as they take more responsibility for learning

1

- Empowering teachers to design learning experiences for students instead of relying on textbooks to be the controller of what and how to teach
- Breaking away from bureaucratic structures that inhibit teacher creativity and the willingness to take risks
- Critically examining education at all levels in light of changing paradigms for managing, teaching, and learning

But the fast pace to incorporate new ways of doing business in schools has created some concerns among teachers:

- "How do we know these innovations really make a difference in helping students achieve?"
- "We have so many pieces going on in our school—sometimes it feels like an innovation jigsaw puzzle."
- "We need a system to make sure we have a coherent, articulated, and coordinated plan for our school program."
- "I have concerns about some of the different innovations. Some things just don't feel right."
- "We need more time to think, dialogue, and plan in schools. These changes require ongoing development of people and programs."

Pressure Groups

Add to these concerns the conflicting messages from a society carrying multiple agendas and worldviews, and the job of educational change becomes highly complex. Five of these pressure groups are especially pronounced.

First, there is business and the world of work. They decry the quality of education in America and lament, "If only workers had the skills we need, our companies would be economically competitive in the global marketplace." Business pressures government to make change in schools, and legislation rumbles across the floor with a heavy hand—but a weaker handshake when it comes to funding.

Following suit, state governments set up commissions and panels to evaluate and plan for a restructured system of education. Goals are defined and **standards** are set, and the easy work is completed. Then the burden of proof shifts to the schools and the steeled expectations seem enormous. Somehow it feels in schools as if a critical step has been crossed off the state planning page. Where is the step that supports the school's identified needs (time, training, technology, and the like) so that the outcomes can be met?

The third pressure group is the extreme religious right. Though their support of the family, and of family values, is laudable, their tactics for promoting a fundamentalist agenda for religion in the schools and a narrow focus for **curriculum** are dangerous for a democratic society that is founded on the principles of freedom of religion and speech. Their literature and presentations generate a feeling of public distrust and suspicion toward government and schools.

Because of the conflict between the aims of business, government, and factions of the religious right, many educators are confused. They too often retreat from the controversy and try to avoid any educational terminology that might attract negative attention from extremist groups.

Media is the fourth pressure group. They highlight the negative, whether crime, violence, corruption, or falling standardized test scores. It is interesting that national surveys of parents grade their own child's school as doing an A or B job, but the nation's schools in general are perceived as failing. How great a role does media play in the national view? There are a number of researchers and leaders in education today who are countering this negative barrage—but they are only heard through the educational literature or conferences. Their data supporting the successes of education in America never seem to hit the front pages of newspapers. What if publishers insisted that a positive story in education had to be written for every negative story? The same should occur for our other institutions such as law enforcement and government. I fear that the ongoing negative diatribe is beginning to engender a breakdown of support for, and potential collapse of, our institutional social structure.

The truth is that education does need a new curricular and instructional model, but not because of teacher or administrator failures. The problem is based in rapidly changing societal needs that are centered on economics, demographic factors, and politics. We have a systems problem. The old system of education is not functional for delivering the highly cognitive, conceptual, and technical skills that are needed for the 21st century.

Many of the current trends in education reflect the increasing complexity caused by the growing interdependence of diverse elements. Educationally responsive trends such as "Integrated Curriculum," "multicultural education," "inclusion," "multiage," and "cooperative learning" share the common thread of *diversity working together.* New skills for bringing structure and manageability to complex and diverse systems are now required in life and work roles.

Advances in technology, the growth of knowledge, and the mobility of world populations have dramatically altered the simple lifestyles of an earlier age. Required worker and social skills are complex and sophisticated. Schools reflect the changing requirements.

In addition to the need to meet the requirements of complex life roles, education helps diverse systems work together to bring structure to seeming curricular chaos caused by fragmentation. For example, even though disciplines retain a separate structure, bringing the viewpoints together to look at complex issues, questions, or concepts in an integrated fashion brings focus to learning. Complex questions require broader perspectives. The more complex the question, the higher the levels of required cognitive abstraction to see the critical connections.

Educational change will only occur in a cooperative, problem-solving partnership with business, the community, and parents. The current aura of blaming impedes progress by generating feelings of hopelessness. By addressing the needs at the building level, supporting teachers and administrators, dialoguing as a community, and addressing the desired student outcomes with an analytical systems approach, we can align public schooling with societal and individual needs.

The final pressure group, and the one that I feel the most concern for, is the parents. What a confusing time for them! Between the mixed messages coming from media, business, the extreme religious right, and the schools, parents often don't know what to think. No wonder so many parents are opting for private or home schooling. Never before has the need to include parents in the educational setting been more urgent.

Sharing the Job of Quality Education

Parents as Partners

Parents need to understand the changing world and how education is working to provide students with the skills for success in the 21st century. Progressive schools cooperatively plan the educational program with parents and see that they are involved in the educational process whether at the school site or as support to their children at home.

Traditionally in education we have opened our doors only slightly to parents. We have engaged them as volunteers for various activities but have had difficulty communicating our plan for learning. Today, educators must find ways to include parents in defining the aims of education and show how the school learning plan is focused toward achieving those aims. Parents want and deserve to be active partners in their children's educational experience.

Parents are feeling heightened anxiety for the safety as well as the education of their children. In a society that is increasingly violent and threatening, and in which guns appear to be as plentiful as bubble gum, parents naturally hold their children close. They want to see plans to ensure the safety and well-being of children in school. This must be an issue for the community as well as the school.

Community and Business as Partners

Education is a community venture with schools, churches, health, welfare, and law enforcement agencies working together to provide for the needs of children. In some communities, there are excellent communication networks between the public agencies. Help to families is focused and timely. In other communities, there is a breakdown in relationships. Families wait months for assistance from overburdened caseworkers or suffer from duplication of effort between agencies.

One model that appears particularly effective in a small community in Montana calls together an interagency task force, which includes representatives from the schools, health and human service agencies, law enforcement, and the clergy. This task force meets on a monthly basis to dialogue and develop ways to more effectively and efficiently serve the many families they share. Task force members become acquainted as professionals and open lines of communication to efficiently serve individual families.

Business, as another important segment of the community, also has an important role in education. Certainly many of the requested changes in schooling are emanating from the needs of business. But their advertisements calling for change are sometimes disturbing.

The National Business Roundtable advertises that "America has failed its children in education." Educators remind the Roundtable that schools were modeled after industry 40 years ago to efficiently produce workers who knew some basic facts and followed orders. But today, business has changed their requirements for education. Now they need workers who can access, process, and use knowledge in the solution of complex problems while working as members of a team.

Instead of acknowledging that the needs of business have become more sophisticated, however, and offering full support to help restructure schools, educators feel that business points the finger in blame, which serves to undermine public confidence in a critical American institution. Most educators support the requests of business to alter the educational program. But they would like to feel a spirit of full cooperation and support as they build a fleet of roadsters out of a string of factory-designed bumper cars.

There are many businesses around the country providing positive support to schools through business partnerships. These businesses aid schools through activities such as allowing employees to speak to classes during the workday or providing funding to support the development of technology in schools. The business world wants technologically literate workers, but computers and more advanced technologies are in scarce supply in most schools. Helping schools solve the problem of an *inadequate* and *inequitable* supply of technology would be one of the best ways for businesses to help boost school change into the 21st century.

The Dilemma of Time and Funding

. . . in a Minute . . . with a Nickel

There are policymakers who have difficulty understanding why education is so slow to change. They believe that if tests are developed for students and high stakes are set for both students and schools, the change process will occur naturally. But educators know that these changes are a major transformation in outcomes, teaching paradigms, techniques, and materials. They require long-term cooperation and commitment for training and funding.

Dr. Willard Daggett, the head of Vocational Education and Language Arts for the state of New York in 1991, stated in a speech at that time, "American Education is using a rearview mirror approach to curriculum and instruction. We do what we have always done, because that is what we know." One of our most difficult tasks in designing a more meaningful school program will be to critically assess what we have always done and resist old patterns that rob valuable time from new directions.

Two examples come to mind to demonstrate the complexity of curricular and instructional change. The first one deals with the process of curriculum development. Some districts follow the dictates of the textbook for their curriculum. Others attempt to write their own curriculum and then adopt a textbook to meet defined objectives. But the process too often breaks down because the teachers write a curriculum that looks suspiciously like the textbook they just completed teaching. They write what they know.

The second example revolves around the definition of *depth of instruction*. Under the older fact-based paradigm, *depth of instruction* meant *teaching more facts about a topic*. In the newer paradigm, depth of instruction means *teaching higher level thinking related to a significant concept and theme, problem, or issue by connecting ideas across disciplines to extend understanding, find answers, foster* **generalizations,** and create new knowledge. This shift in definition highlights the complex change in instruction as teachers challenge their own thinking so as to facilitate student thinking. Content serves not as an end product but as a tool for thought and action.

The increasing emphasis on critical and creative thinking in schooling requires a level of staff development that goes far beyond "make it and take it" workshops or five early release day presentations by experts. The level of staff development that is necessary to effect the needed changes in curriculum, instruction, and systems planning is ongoing and weekly. If the United States is serious about wanting an improved educational system, we will evaluate the time needed for teachers and administrators to interact as professionals in learning new skills. We must bring teachers out of the individual boxes and provide them with the time for collegial study and dialogue.

I have seen the greatest school improvements when teachers and administrators are given time to deal intellectually and in depth with the essential questions related to their profession in a changing world. The school year should be extended so that teachers and administrators have one morning per week for professional dialogue, curriculum writing, and staff development. It is critical that educators be accountable for the use of this time, however, by showing results to their community.

It is important to hold the staff/curriculum development time in the morning. Some schools are following a model of early release days, but I have found this model to be insufficient. It is often only an hour or an hour and a half long. This is too short a time to complete any meaningful dialogue or work. Some teachers also feel compelled to attend to other business during that time, which erodes the school-based, professional focus.

The high level of staff development and curriculum work to be undertaken during the professional development time requires alert minds. The higher the quality of thinking that is brought to planning, the better the program for students. Results should show for students by the second year if time is used well.

Numerous schools in states such as Washington, Oregon, Florida, and Alaska are now banking time by extending the school day for a few minutes and shortening the passing time between classes. Banked time is turned into a three-hour-late-arrival day on alternating weeks. The complexity of schooling today requires this professional use of time for dialogue, training, and curriculum development. We will not see the kind of school transformation we are seeking without this change. Teachers in Germany and Japan have longer school years but have much less contact time with students during the day. They have the time to dialogue and learn together.

Big business recognizes the need for quality training of their employees. Education is one of the largest businesses, and the job is human development. This job is far more complex than following a standard blueprint to build a standard product. The job of human development takes the individual child in whatever form and guides and nurtures the mind, body, and self-concept. If we raise the expectations for teachers and administrators, then we owe them the training to meet the changing requirements. We get what we pay for. If we expect major change, *in a minute, with a nickel,* we will get what we paid for—*minute change.*

Making Change the Systems Way

Senge and Systems Thinking

A recommended book for all policymakers, leaders, and organizations interested in change is *The Fifth Discipline* by Peter Senge (1990). Central to Senge's thesis is the view that

> learning organizations . . . where people continually expand their capacity to create the results they truly desire, where new and expansive patterns of thinking are nurtured, where collective aspiration is set free, and where people are continually learning how to learn together . . . develop in a culture which embraces systems thinking. (p. 2)

Systems thinking, states Senge, is a framework for looking at the interrelationships and patterns of change over time. Too often, events are perceived in isolation, and quick fixes for symptoms are applied. Systems thinking is the "integrating discipline" for seeing the underlying structures that need to be considered in making change (Senge, 1990, p. 69).

Senge calls the critical components for a learning organization "disciplines." The first four disciplines—"Personal Mastery, Mental Models, Building Shared Vision, and Team Learning"—are integrated through the fifth discipline, "Systems Thinking." Senge (1990, pp. 7-10) gives the following definitions:

- *Personal Mastery:* The discipline of continually clarifying and deepening our personal vision, of focusing our energies, of developing patience, and of seeing reality objectively
- *Mental Models:* Deeply ingrained assumptions, generalizations, or even pictures or images that influence how we understand the world and how we take action
- *Building Shared Vision:* The capacity to build and hold a shared picture of the future we seek to create

  - People with shared vision have genuine commitment and enrollment rather than compliance.

- *Team Learning:* The ability to dialogue and suspend assumptions while entering into a genuine "thinking together"

  - Team learning also involves learning how to recognize the patterns of interaction in teams that undermine learning.

A major difficulty in the restructuring of schools is a lack of the five disciplines in action. People work in their comfort zone, each tinkering with a piece of the whole. But a coordinated, systemic plan for change is too often absent. Policymakers insist on tests; assessment people comply. Principals encourage teachers to risk and try new ideas; teachers comply. A plethora of new buzzword innovations sweep into classrooms but are seldom evaluated for their contributions to increased student success. Teachers and principals request time to dialogue, plan, and design effective programs, but there is a breakdown in the system, because this essential need remains but a whisper at the budget and policy tables. It is feared that parents would never support the scheduling change. It is time to let parents in on the complexity of the change being asked of us. It is time to gain support for these reasonable requests for time.

The five disciplines as defined by Senge are about professional communication, interaction, and development. Learning organizations will be as effective as their wise and focused use of precious time in cultivating these five disciplines.

Overcoming Obstacles:
Over, Under, Through, and Around

Educators have an indomitable spirit. In spite of a lack of coordinated problem solving and systems thinking in school districts, teachers and administrators strive to improve education for the students in their school. A powerful point made by Senge is that learning organizations move forward on the collective vision and actions of people. They overcome obstacles and achieve their goals because they are all headed in the same direction, toward a shared vision (Senge, 1990).

The problem we face in improving education is not a matter of dealing with inertia. There is plenty of activity. The problem is that the activity, or innovation, is often not part of a comprehensive and shared vision. The innovation may give a false sense of accomplishment because it is new, but the question hangs in the air, "Does this innovation make a difference in achieving the desired outcomes for students?"

Innovation and change need to be viewed in the context of systems improvement. Schools can have the best curricular plan for students, but if there is no allowance for teacher and principal training on the curriculum, student assessment to check for progress, and program evaluation to see what works and what doesn't, then the system breaks down.

Systems thinking looks at all players. When business works with government to require certain outcomes from schools, then business becomes part of the system. Parents, too, are part of the system. So are the community agencies that support children and families. It is time for each of the players to stop pushing buttons in isolation and begin working together, using systems thinking, so that the positive and negative patterns of school change can be identified. Then, we hope, random activities can be focused toward a common vision in each school, and success for all students can become reality.

Obstacles do not stop progress in a school or district that has a clear vision, broad support and understanding, and a systems approach to change. Obstacles become merely problems to solve and serve as an opportunity to reflect on even better ways of operating. Critical to a strong system, however, is the development of leaders—those people who conceptualize, mobilize, clarify, and support.

Leaders of Change

District curriculum leaders can be teachers, principals, or central office people in charge of programs. This discussion is focused on curriculum leaders, but the characteristics and abilities that are presented apply generally to all leaders in organizations.

Leadership as an art calls for a keen *sensitivity* to human behavior and interpersonal exchange. Leaders hold in-depth knowledge but *respect* the group process. They know when to lead and offer information, when to support, and when to follow. They are *critical and creative thinkers* and have the *intellectual capacity* to synthesize, abstract, and conceptualize by connecting key thoughts and ideas. Leaders have *strong communication skills.* They move people to action with clear and compelling thoughts and ideas. They bring promise to problems.

Leadership, Intellect, and Thought

Curriculum leaders are faced with an array of innovative trends, whether "**Whole Language,**" "**constructivist** learning environments," "site-based management," or "Outcome-Based Education." For each trend, a continuum of implementation models develop. On one end are the innovation purists who envision the idea in its extreme. The purists usually give little credence to what they perceive as the tainted models on the opposite end of the continuum. The converse is also true. The extreme traditionalists may begrudgingly buy a tad of the innovative philosophy. Their model is comfort, with a piece of innovation tacked on.

Strong curriculum leaders move out of the comfort zone, but they do not jump into the innovation swim without first testing the current. They ask critical questions:

- Is this innovation really new, or is it a replay of a time gone by?
- If it is a replay, what is different this time around? What do history and research say about its potential for helping students become more successful?
- What do we know about these ideas?
- What more do we need to learn?
- How will this innovation fit into our system? Does our system need to change?

  - What changes will we need to make in organizational structures, curriculum, instruction, delivery models, governance, and so on?

- How can we best use resources to achieve the desired changes?
- What forms of monitoring will be employed to ensure that the innovation is truly making a difference in the success of students?

Sometimes districts mandate the innovative philosophy without considering the ramifications. There is great interest today, for example, in site-based management and site-based decision making. As with so many trends, districts buy the reasonable theory, "We have to break the bureaucratic district structure," and "Let's get decision making and the money as close to the classroom as possible."

Then the different models for site-based management begin to emerge. Some are purist forms: Central office program positions are disbanded; district program budgets are dispersed to the buildings; each school buys its own staff development, writes and purchases curricula of its choice, designs and monitors special education and federally funded programs; and so on. What starts as an empowering idea suddenly turns into a nightmare in many schools. The quantum leap, without appropriate discussion and planning regarding the needed support structures, creates chaos and frustration at the building level.

The problems that have developed in these purist leaps of faith are based on a set of faulty assumptions (see Table 1.1).

Historically, bureaucratic structures have admittedly been a major problem in positive school change:

- Teachers had little input into the design of curriculum.
- Funding support for classroom materials and innovation too often remained at the mercy of top-level managers who had no understanding of curricular and instructional needs related to students.
- Communication bottlenecks occurred because people couldn't, or wouldn't, convey needs, plans, and ideas.

But wise curriculum leaders and school district managers are moving cautiously toward site-based management. They strive for balance and work to clearly define roles, responsibilities, and functions between central office and site-based personnel. They look at all elements of the school system to make certain that supports for areas such as staff development, teaming, leadership training, policy, governance issues, and resource allocations are all considered in short- and long-range planning. They ask critical questions, such as the following:

- What evidence will assure us that site-based management is improving the education for all students? They hear the business world state, "What education needs is competition between the schools." But they realize that the collapse of a company that deals in lifeless products is very different than the collapse of a school that houses precious human beings.
- Is the idea of a deregulated market for schools really a viable answer? Or will it simply mean a few winners and many marked failures with nowhere for the losers to go?

Table 1.1. Site-Based Assumptions/Actualities

Assumptions	Actualities
1. Teachers and administrators will have the time to carry out functions that were formerly led by central office program leaders: research, curriculum development, staff development, text and materials review and purchase, special education, program monitoring, and so on.	1. Finding enough time for professional work is always a problem in schools. Teachers and administrators do not want to have all of the responsibilities from central office. They want a flexible framework that will allow them to be creative and critical thinkers within a reasonable district structure.
2. School site personnel have the knowledge and skills to design and deliver a quality educational program for the 21st century.	2. Some schools have personnel with the knowledge and skills that are needed, but many teachers and administrators find it difficult to stay current with the research and professional literature because of time constraints, evening work from school, and family responsibilities.
3. School sites have the leadership required for effecting major curricular and instructional change.	3. Some school sites have quality leaders whether in the principal or teachers, but too often the requisite knowledge, skills, attitudes, and abilities for leading the change effort have not been developed in the traditionally controlled environment.
4. Schooling will improve dramatically if left to site-based management.	4. This has not been proven. There is the potential to improve dramatically, as long as the other system components provide support: time to plan and design, budgetary support, district-level support, and parental support. Too often, the system supports are weak or missing, and only a few vocal schools seem to get the needed aid.

- Instead of a focus on competition and a game of winners and losers, wouldn't a systemic, rather than a competitive, approach to the creation of a nation of winning schools be more appropriate?

Wise leaders question further:

- If each school were to develop and choose its own curricular program, what would the effect be, districtwide?
- How can we continually build the capacity in our personnel, at each building site, to conceptualize, plan, and design a relevant curricular and instructional program for the 21st century?
- How far do we want to move on the continuum toward site-based management? Should we progress in that direction in proportion to the readiness of the personnel and community to effectively manage the change?
- Can we balance the functions between central office and the school sites so that we remove the traditional blocks to school progress but build a much stronger school "system"?
- Can we have a district core curriculum, developed by districtwide teacher committees, that supports the district philosophy and graduating student outcomes but that gives individual school sites wide autonomy in curriculum delivery methods, school structures, and expenditure of school budgets?

Whatever the innovation, thoughtful leaders of change ask and answer many critical questions before they move large groups of people forward. They dialogue with others and seek answers until they are comfortable that the direction is sound and appropriate for their district or school. They may not have all of the answers but will have achieved a trusting level of comfort about the overall direction. Leaders listen to their inner voice, which is tied to their comfort levels, on when and how to proceed. They will not have all of the information, but they will recognize when they have enough information to move forward.

Not having all of the answers is a common state for leaders. It is to be expected. Good leaders live easily with ambiguity, for they are confident that answers will come in time. It is important for leaders to be relaxed with ambiguity, for they will need to reassure others. Sometimes educators become stressed when all of the answers to their questions regarding an innovation are not readily apparent. They are used to working in a system where routine is established and expectations leave little room for new directions. In these cases, ambiguity is felt as a situational loss of control.

Effective curriculum leaders weigh innovation against their experience, knowledge, and societal and student needs. They often adapt a popular innovation—taking the best and tossing the rest. They work with teacher, parent, and administrator committees to shape a curricular program that meets the needs of the students and local community. They know that a systems design for curriculum and instruction is not built on others' innovations alone.

Creative leaders see the bigger picture and lead people to build a collaborative vision of what needs to be. The ability to conceptualize new forms for teaching and learning and the ability to see details as integral parts of a whole design are key characteristics of quality leadership. Building a vision involves asking the right questions at the appropriate time, clarifying ideas, and summarizing directions.

Leadership, Respect, and Sensitivity

Quality designs for curriculum and instruction emerge in safe environments of thoughtful risk taking. Safe environments are created when there is respect for the group process and the participating individuals. Leaders set a tone for comfort, respect, and colleagueship.

Curriculum leaders clearly outline a problem or task, and then flexibly shift among roles. They are sensitive to the thoughts and feelings that emerge from the group and use a number of roles to guide the process:

- *Clarifier:* Drawing out the critical questions that need to be addressed in solving the problem or doing the task; seeking clarification of group members' ideas; ensuring that all are clear on the issues and solutions

- *Definer:* Drawing out an array of solutions from the group with a display of the benefits and drawbacks of each
- *Mediator:* Listening, clarifying, finding common ground in disparate views; being sensitive to interpersonal feelings and interactions and valuing all contributions
- *Coach:* Explaining and sharing when there are gaps in knowledge; motivating, enlisting, and, at times, directing when tasks need to be completed; maintaining the group focus for task completion
- *Tone setter:* Creating a task orientation with high expectations for quality, set in an atmosphere of light humor, personal acknowledgment, trust, and respect

Effective leaders do not bring a committee together to write curriculum without a clear understanding of the task to be accomplished and a workable design for writing. Time is valuable in schools and teachers expect curricular leaders to have at least an idea of a workable writing format. The format can be revised, if necessary, as the process of writing ensues. The writing format can be developed with a prior subcommittee meeting. Time is saved and used more productively when the curriculum leader or subcommittee has practiced using the writing format prior to the actual committee work. This step points out problems or questions that are likely to arise in the large committee and allows them to be addressed as a part of the task training.

Leadership and Communication

Perhaps the key leadership quality is communication. Effective communication is derived from all of the other leadership components:

- *depth of knowledge*—a command of different domains of information
- *intellectual capacity*—critical and creative thought; systems thinking

- *sensitivity*—an intuitive feel for individual actions and reactions in interpersonal settings
- *respect*—a belief and trust in the thoughts, ideas, and work of others

Communication is often cited as the area of breakdown in organizational systems. Lack of effective communication networks in school systems is a major reason for the push toward site-based management. The distance from the classroom to the budget table, for example, is too great. People in high positions make decisions to cut school programs and materials without understanding the full impact of those decisions on the students in the classroom. With the costs continually rising for heat and lights, the discretionary funds in curriculum and school budgets become vulnerable.

The importance of effective communication for curriculum leaders cannot be overstated. Organizational communication is dependent on the quality of the communication between leaders in the organization—and between the leaders and the people who are working with them. Some curriculum leaders make assumptions about the level of understanding and support for a curricular innovation. They may fail to clearly articulate and dialogue with teachers, and the plan for change falls through.

Another common communication error is failing to show clearly how an innovation fits into the total curricular and instructional system. Teachers soon feel as if they are running a three-ring circus of disjointed innovations. That is a common complaint in districts across the United States today: "I don't see how all of these innovations fit together!"

Clear communication related to curriculum means thinking through the issues prior to a presentation and asking the planning questions:

- "Who is my audience?"
- "What will they want to know?"
- "What will their concerns be? How will I address those concerns?"
- "What are the key points that need to be made?"

- "How can I show the relationship of the innovations or ideas to the total system of curriculum and instruction in the district?"
- "How much time will I have for the presentation?"
- "How can I effectively communicate the ideas so that my audience is comfortable with what they hear?"
- "How can I engage the audience with the innovation or its adaptation so that they have opportunities to build ownership?"

The Dilemmas of Curricular Planning

Voices Along a Continuum

Depending on which educational expert you listen to at national conferences today, you will hear one of three messages:

- "We are losing our cultural heritage. We must focus on creating a fundamental body of knowledge in schools."
- "Facts are only important as tools for developing lifelong learning **process skills.** Students need to focus not on memorization of content but on developing the ability to access, ponder, and create knowledge."
- "Content and process are both important but must be brought into a better balance in the school curriculum."

Educators, parents, and communities need to think critically about each of these statements, ask questions and discuss answers, and then decide on a philosophical direction for their schools. Each of the messages delivers a very different systems design package to a school or district curricular program.

Designing a Systems Plan for Curriculum

My bias is that the popular opinion in education usually swings to the extremes, and balance is better. Therefore I would propose that both content and process are important in the school curriculum. A focus on memorizing trails of trivia will do little to develop independent thinkers who take responsibility for learning and are motivated to search for knowledge. Nor will a focus on process skills for lifelong learning have much meaning if students have not formed a mental schema for categorizing the mass of information that rises to greet them.

A systems plan for curriculum values both knowing and doing. It ensures that process and content work together in an articulated and coordinated framework. A systems design for schools does not support each school in a district bounding off in a different curricular direction. It works through a committee process to develop a common framework for the district curriculum from elementary through the secondary levels. The framework does not list low-level content objectives with process verbs identified for each piece of content. But it does include the following components:

- A district mission statement and philosophy
- District Student Outcomes (five or six broad statements of what students will know and be able to do by graduation)
- Program (subject area) Outcomes and **benchmark** performances from grades K to 12
- The key concepts and critical content, listed by topics or thematic units, that form the core content curriculum at each grade level, or grade band
- Scope and sequence charts for the process development areas only—reading, writing, mathematics

  - Scope and sequence charts assist teachers in knowing when to introduce developmental strategies and skills. These charts, however, are not as detailed as the behaviorally designed scope and sequence charts of the 1970s and 1980s.

- A plan for measuring progress through the grades on the District Student Outcomes

  - **Performance assessments,** for example, measure what students know and are able to do.

The Teacher as Lead Designer

Curriculum frameworks are necessary because each teacher is only one partner in the educational process. Teachers form a nurturing chain for students as they move through the grades. It is necessary to have a coordinated and articulated plan for fostering student development.

The main function of curriculum frameworks or guides is to assist teachers with their planning. The teacher is the lead designer for curriculum and instruction in the classroom. Frameworks need to be written so that teachers have wide latitude in the design and delivery of the curricular program.

The ability to think critically and creatively is an important outcome of schooling for the 21st century. Thinking teachers develop thinking students. If we believe that allowing students to take more responsibility for their learning will stimulate their cognitive abilities, then we realize that allowing teachers to take responsibility for the design and delivery of curriculum will likewise challenge their cognitive abilities.

Chapter 2 looks at some of the desired schooling outcomes that communities hold for their children. School systems need to hold the same outcomes for staff. Thinking teachers who are globally aware, who communicate at high levels, who take responsibility for their actions, and who relate well interpersonally provide the best instruction and models for a progressive education.

SUMMARY

The complexity of educational change in a rapidly changing world sends confusing messages to schools. The requirements for change, to meet the needs of society and students, call for highly trained teachers and administrators. This job cannot be done effectively without providing quality time each week for professional dialogue, training of staff, and curriculum development. Teachers need to learn new skills for the changing role of schools.

A committed partnership between schools, parents, business, and the community is essential to a quality plan for education. A systems approach to the education of each child brings the parts into a coherent whole—and the children are the winners.

All organizational systems have leaders—people who have the ability to analyze, synthesize, and conceptualize. People who know when to speak and when to listen, when to lead and when to follow. Leadership is an ability to empower others, which multiplies the positive effects of change tenfold.

Leadership, system support, and teacher empowerment are critical to positive educational change. Teachers need flexibility and support to design and deliver the classroom program for students using curricular frameworks as a guide.

The purpose of educational change is to achieve student success as defined in part by graduation Outcomes. Change just for the sake of change is wheel spinning. Change for the sake of children is our job.

Extending Thought

1. Why must education become a community partnership in the systems view?
2. What questions should parents ask of educators today?
3. How would you respond to those questions as an educator?
4. The dilemmas of little time and short funding are school realities. How can you creatively and practically "make time" and "find funding"?
5. How can you use the power of motivation to overcome most obstacles to educational change efforts?
6. How would you characterize "leadership"?

CHAPTER **2**

How Societal Trends
Shape Student Outcomes

R apidly changing demographic factors, economics, and politics call for self-directed learners who show responsibility for
themselves and their local and world communities. Global
perspectives and understanding, the ability to communicate clearly,
and the ability to relate well interpersonally are critical in a multicultural society and a technology-oriented, world marketplace. Curricula for the future emphasize the learner's development as much as
the content to be learned. Critical and creative thinking serve as the
point, and counterpoint, as students construct knowledge using
multiple perspectives, talents, modalities, and mediums.

Relevant curricula related to life and our world encourage depth
over coverage in course content and an interdisciplinary integration
of skills, concepts, and information. Some curricula draw lessons
from the past; all curricula prepare students for the future.

An Eye to the Future

Trends

Curriculum developers become effective "trend readers" in providing relevant preparation for the 21st century. They rise above the data related to social, economic, and political change and view the bigger picture. How do the trends relate and influence each other? What are the projected system changes? And, importantly, what skills, knowledge, attitudes, and abilities must students and staff possess to operate successfully in these changing systems?

An overarching framework for world change is the *globalization of economics and trade*, stimulated by *advances in technology, transportation*, and *world democratization*. To successfully prepare our young people to live and work within globally networked systems, curriculum developers listen to business and economic futurists.

The Global Economy

The famed economist Lester Thurow, in his provocative and thoughtful book *Head to Head: The Coming Economic Battle Among Japan, Europe, and America* (1993), outlines clearly the emerging economic contest. In the European community and Japan, where the United States has reigned supreme for the past 50 years as the economic power, it is now jockeying into a competitive/cooperative relationship. The coalition of western European countries into a powerful economic unit is not yet complete, but it is only a matter of time.

Thurow (1993) cites the following questions as central to the developing economic competition:

> Who can make the best products? Who expands their standard of living most rapidly? Who has the best-educated and best-skilled work force in the world? Who is the world's leader in investment—plant and equipment, research and development (R&D), infrastructure? Who organizes best? Whose institutions—government, education, business—are world leaders in efficiency? (p. 23)

A critical factor for American companies in the coming economic competition will be the facility with which workers learn the new technologies. Thurow points out that the leading industries of the future are all "brainpower industries." Microelectronics, biotechnology, new materials industries, civilian aviation, telecommunication, robotics plus machine tools, and computers plus software involve high-skill jobs. Businesses who master the high-tech process technologies will have the advantage in economic competition in the 21st century. The skills of the labor force will be the key competitive weapon of the future, and American companies will be at a distinct disadvantage if their workers take longer to learn the new technologies (Thurow, 1993, pp. 51-54).

Competitive foreign firms in Germany and Japan have invested their monetary resources heavily in the training of workers and in the processes of product development. American firms have traditionally been more concerned with product than process. With the globalization of the economy and the increasing international competition for jobs, we cannot afford to ignore the development of our greatest resource—our people.

Will the traditional U.S. curriculum provide the competitive skills that our workforce needs? Not by a long shot; but educators are coming to that realization. The insular schoolhouse is difficult to crack, but small advances are taking place.

The rapid changes occurring in the workplace are affecting the curriculum of vocational programs by emphasizing problem solving, teamwork, and the use of technology in conjunction with "real-world" simulations and experiences. Robotics, bridge building, laser applications, and CO_2 cars are replacing birdhouses and boxes in the vocational classroom. The critical need for a quality workforce has been a major impetus for the development of high-level student outcomes in the traditionally differentiated academic and vocational classrooms. The current trends to reinforce school-to-work transitions will have a tremendous impact on the secondary school curriculum. Model programs blending vocational and academic programming are popping up around the country, through **career paths**, applied academics programs, and tech prep programs.

Educators are engaging students in activities that help them take more responsibility for constructing knowledge and using it to solve problems related to life role issues. Teachers are eager to learn new ways of teaching that will help students develop higher skill levels. But organizational problems of time, focus, and funding still impede effective teacher training. In schools, we need highly trained, thinking teachers if we want high-performing, thinking students. Our future will accept no less.

The Global Labor Market

William B. Johnston, in an article for the *Harvard Business Review* titled "Global Work Force 2000: The New World Labor Market" (1991), speaks to the growing mobility of the workforce and states that the future will increasingly bring a world market for labor. Employers are searching the globe for workers with the needed skills. In the United States, the business community laments the shortage of qualified workers. While industrialized nations strive to find skilled workers, the developing nations are producing a surplus of workers for their economies. The results, according to Johnston, will include mass migrations of people, especially the young, educated workers who will look for employment in the developed countries of the world. There will be international competition for the most highly skilled global citizens (Johnston, 1991).

The U.S. Secretary of Labor formed a commission called SCANS, the Secretary's Commission on Achieving Necessary Skills (1991), to investigate what is required in today's and tomorrow's workplace and to determine the readiness of our high school students to meet those requirements. In June 1991 the commission issued a report that identified five competencies for workplace success. Figure 2.1 outlines the SCANS competencies.

The SCANS competencies have little to do with the traditional content of schooling. They are high-level personal competencies, and it is apparent they are the kinds of skills and aptitudes that make or break a worker. More people lose jobs because of poorly developed competence in these areas than because of a lack of content knowledge. It is also evident that these are leadership competencies. This means that workers of the future must be independent thinkers, as well as team problem solvers, and should not expect to wait for the answers from a superior.

Resources: Identifies, organizes, and allocates resources

A. Time—Selects goal-relevant activities, ranks them, allocates time, and prepares and follows schedules
B. Money—Uses or prepares budgets, makes forecasts, keeps records, and makes adjustments to meet objectives
C. Material and Facilities—Acquires, stores, allocates, and uses materials or space efficiently
D. Human Resources—Assesses skills and distributes work accordingly, evaluates performance, and provides feedback

Information: Acquires and uses information

A. Acquires and evaluates information
B. Organizes and maintains information
C. Interprets and communicates information
D. Uses computers to process information

Interpersonal: Works with others

A. Participates as Member of a Team—Contributes to group effort
B. Teaches Others New Skills
C. Serves Clients/Customers—Works to satisfy customers' expectations
D. Exercises Leadership—Communicates ideas to justify position, persuades and convinces others, responsibly challenges existing procedures and policies
E. Negotiates—Works toward agreements involving exchange of resources,   resolves divergent interests
F. Works with Diversity—Works well with men and women from diverse backgrounds

Systems: Understands complex interrelationships

A. Understands Systems: Knows how social, organizational, and technological systems work and operates effectively in them
B. Monitors and Corrects Performance—Distinguishes trends, predicts impacts on system operations, diagnoses deviations in systems' performance, and corrects malfunctions
C. Improves or Designs Systems—Suggests modifications to existing systems and develops new or alternative systems to improve performance

Technology: Works with a variety of technologies

A. Selects Technology—Chooses procedures, tools or equipment, including computers and related technologies
B. Applies Technology to Task—Understands overall intent and proper procedures for setup and operation of equipment
C. Maintains and Troubleshoots Equipment—Prevents, identifies, or solves problems with equipment, including computers and other technologies

Figure 2.1. SCANS Competencies
SOURCE: U.S. Department of Labor.

Salable Skills in the Global Market

In *The Work of Nations,* U.S. Secretary of Labor Robert Reich (1992) reminds us that schools in the 1950s reflected the national economy, with "a standard assembly-line curriculum divided neatly into subjects, taught in predictable units of time, arranged sequentially by grade, and controlled by standardized tests intended to weed out defective units and return them for reworking" (p. 226).

Reich's book outlines the transformation from a national to a global economy and states that by the 1990s the average American student will be ill-equipped to compete in the global economy. He presents the argument that Americans can no longer depend on major corporations and industries for personal and national economic security and success. Their success will depend instead on their personal ability to add to the global economy through their skills and insights.

Reich groups the majority of American jobs into three broad categories of contribution to the global economy. The first two categories are "routine production services" and "in-person services" (Reich, 1992, pp. 174-176). Routine production services encompass jobs that require repetitive routine, from assembly line workers to low- and middle-level supervisors who routinely check work and procedures of subordinates. Routine production services do not require high levels of education.

In-person services also encompass simple and repetitive tasks. They do not require education beyond high school, except perhaps some vocational training. In-person service workers, such as waiters, janitors, secretaries, or security guards, interact directly with their customers (Reich, 1992).

Neither category will earn as high a wage as the third category—that of the "symbolic analysts." According to Reich (1992, pp. 229-232), symbolic analysts exhibit and refine four basic skills:

- *Abstraction*—discovering patterns and meanings; using models, constructing analogies, equations, and metaphors in order to make sense, rearranging and creating new possibilities from the mass of information available
- *System thinking*—seeing reality as a system of interacting causes, consequences, and relationships

- *Experimentation*—applying thought and reason while systematically exploring different options in testing ideas and intuition
  against past results and assumptions
- *Collaboration*—working in groups to plan and solve problems;
  using the key skills of collaboration: communicating abstract
  ideas, using effective group process techniques, and achieving
  consensus on direction

Reich states that it is not necessarily the job title that determines
whether a person will have salable skills in the global marketplace;
it is the degree to which a worker exhibits the skills of abstraction,
systems thinking, experimentation, and collaboration. Secretaries
can be symbolic analysts if they perform with the high-level skills,
and lawyers can be routine production workers if they churn out
standard forms with little thought. Generally, however, the college-
educated students will be better positioned for entering the competitive global market (Reich, 1992).

As educators, we must prepare students with the skills of the
symbolic analyst to have them realize their unique potential, to
prevent the growing disparity between rich and poor, and to preserve
a healthy national economy. What changes need to occur in curriculum and instruction to develop these highly valued skills in our
students? The following chapters on concept-based and **integrated
curriculum** provide methods for structuring the design of curriculum so that the higher level skills, as outlined by Reich, will become
a natural context for teaching and learning.

The ability to see patterns, possibilities, interactions, and relationships, to test ideas and theories, and to experience the power of a
collaborative group process will not be accomplished through the
traditional didactic lecture. Students need to feel personally involved
in the learning experience. The most effective learning occurs when
students engage their minds, bodies, and souls in meaningful studies
and projects. When students are challenged to extend their thoughts
individually, and in a group of learners, they experience a feeling of
involvement that is self-motivating. Our task in education is to
challenge all students to a high level of personal motivation.

More than ever before, teachers need to hold a clear vision for the
teaching/learning process and a solid belief in the ability of all

students to succeed. They must hold the vision in spite of the growing complexity of forces pressing on schools.

Social Trends

In addition to the pressure from business, schools are affected by social forces: increasing immigration that brings many cultures and languages into the classroom, AIDS, drugs and alcohol, and increasing poverty and violence among children.

The United Nations International Children's Emergency Fund issued a report in the fall of 1993, *The Progress of Nations* (cited in the *Seattle Times*, September 26, 1993), stating that the U.S. homicide rate for young people ages 15 to 24 is five times that of its nearest competitor, Canada. Nine out of ten young people murdered in industrialized countries are killed in the United States. For young men of color, the homicide rate is particularly alarming. For all of our talk of equal opportunity and the American dream, we are failing a large segment of our young people, and the consequences sting the conscience.

The UNICEF report goes on to say that child poverty in the United States has increased from 15% in 1970 to 20% in 1992. The poverty rate for children in the United States is more than double that of any other major industrialized nation. Among the 10 wealthiest nations, only the United States and the United Kingdom have experienced declines in the social health indicators of children. Out of 27 industrialized nations, the United States ranks 19th in infant survival rates. The mortality rates among African American infants run high at 18 per 1,000 births. At a time when schools are being called on to educate all children to high standards, the inequality at the starting gate is glaring.

Another factor in the growing poverty rate is the large increase in immigration to the United States. With 1.2 million legal and illegal immigrants coming across our borders each year, we are feeling the effects on schools and social systems. The seeds for conflict are present in a strained economy that already does not employ all of its citizens. But increasing migration of peoples worldwide is a reality. Will our country address the questions related to an increasingly diverse population? Will we ensure adequate support for educational and social systems as they work to support and enculturate new immigrants? Will we address the problems of crime, poverty, joblessness, and inequality of educational opportunity among U.S. citizens? These questions cannot be answered in isolation. They are systemic problems that require creative and coordinated solutions. There is a marked correlation between low educational levels and high poverty and crime rates. Yet education budgets are reduced, while incarceration budgets are increased. We build more prisons, hiding our system failures in concrete boxes. We pay $25,000 per year to hold a prisoner and $4,000 per year to educate a child.

Schools have been thrust to center stage as they wrap their arms around the children of the world. At times, a teacher may have six or more languages and cultures in the classroom. Yet our teachers have had very little training on how to effectively instruct such cultural diversity. Clearly, the schools need to have a focused agenda for meeting the needs of a growing multicultural population. The diversity of America is its greatness. No other country in the world has as rich a diversity in customs, perspectives, values, and beliefs. We can value the diversity and see it as a great opportunity, or we can resist.

International education is a critical element in a future-oriented curriculum. The Eurocentric viewpoint is no longer conscionable as the only perspective to be presented on world issues. As students learn about other cultures, they grow to value diversity as an opportunity for expanded insight and knowledge.

At the same time, schools must teach the values and principles of democracy and a free society. Separating into ethnic enclaves without the common bond of shared beliefs outlined in the U.S. Constitution and the Federalist Papers puts us at risk for the internal ethnic and religious conflict so common in other parts of the world.

Social Change
and the Definition of Curriculum

The definition and orientation of curriculum has evolved over the years as a response to social change and pressures. The following list of forces affecting curriculum, published by the National Center for Research in Vocational Education at the University of California,

Berkeley, represents discussions by futurists, observations from national reports and studies, and reviews of societal trends:

1. Changing family patterns
2. Shifts in the make-up of the labor force
3. Expanding role of technology
4. Changing job demands
5. Increasing global interdependence of people
6. Changing social norms and value structures
7. Worldwide competition and markets
8. Rapid growth of knowledge
9. Ecological concerns
10. Growing demand for an improved educational system (Copa & Pease, 1992, pp. D5-D6)

A New Definition and Model for Curriculum

The complexity of our society, as implied by the 10 major forces cited by Copa and Pease, requires a definition of curriculum that considers the needs of society, the needs of the learner, and the complexity of the learning process. Consistent with these considerations and the model of curriculum being presented in this book, the following definition of curriculum is presented:

CURRICULUM

The planned curriculum is an educational response to the needs of society and the individual, and requires that the learner construct knowledge, attitudes, values, and skills through a complex interplay of mind, materials, and social interactions.

The new view of curriculum recognizes the increasing urgency of societal and human needs. National issues such as pollution and AIDS are also international issues. So, too, are the issues of overpopulation and a healthy economy. These topics of survival are causing nations around the world to plan curricula that lay a foundation for knowledge and lead the learner to problem solve and construct solutions. University professors and high school teachers who gained esteem by being content experts need to help students make the connections between what is known and what is discovered or created. The student who memorizes and recites a complex chemistry formula has *information;* the student who uses the formula to create something new has *knowledge.* You can acquire information by learning facts, but knowledge requires a mental process that connects information to past knowledge and uses the information to construct new realizations.

Student Outcomes

The New Driver for Curriculum

Because of the growing impact from economic, work, and technological and social trends, a national movement to identify graduating "Student Outcomes" shifts the focus of teaching from content to the learner. What students can *do* with what they *know* is the new driver for education. The growing emphasis is on the development of personal process competencies, leading to the attainment of high-level student outcomes by high school graduation. Outcomes such as the ones that follow, stated in many different ways, are causing a redesign of curriculum and instruction in our schools and will be measured developmentally through assessment of performance indicators.

Self-directed learning ability. Technological advances and worldwide interdependence make simple matters complex. The information explosion calls for self-directed learners who can effectively use resources to access critical information, solve problems, create knowledge, and convey thought. Students are active participants in their personal and intellectual development. Through schooling, children learn to be independent decision makers who increasingly take charge of their learning, accept responsibility for managing their lives, and persevere in the resolution of problems. Teachers are facilitators who design the learning environment so that students can construct knowledge and develop their abilities in the performance of challenging tasks. The focus is on the activity of the learner. The teacher becomes a partner in the process of building meaning.

Responsible citizenship. Self-directed learners balance their decisions, exhibiting a sense of responsibility for themselves and their community. The development of a sense of responsibility, although clearly shared by the family and community, is nonetheless an essential part of a school mission. The concept of responsibility includes personal accountability including decision making for health and well-being as well as concern for the welfare of others. Concern for the welfare of others includes the demonstration of respect, concern, and caring. Personal responsibility is *citizenship* in the broadest sense of the term. This means that citizens act to foster the common good, take part in the preservation of democratic processes and principles, and pass on the ideals of life and liberty.

Higher order process skill. Higher order thinkers connect knowledge as they use the information from many different sources and experiences to gain broader perspectives and deeper understanding. They analyze, synthesize, and generalize information as they investigate meaningful problems, issues, and questions. Depth of instruction once meant teaching more facts about a single topic. Today, depth of instruction means teaching higher level, conceptual thinking by connecting ideas across disciplines to extend understanding, foster sound generalizations, and create new knowledge.

Global perspectives and knowledge. Students need opportunities to critically analyze issues from the perspectives of different cultures. The new definition of *social studies*, published in December of 1992 by the National Council for the Social Studies (NCSS, 1992), states that "the primary purpose of social studies is to help young people develop the ability to make informed and reasoned decisions for the public good as citizens of a culturally diverse, democratic society in an interdependent world." James Banks, in a follow-up paper based on his presentation at the American Forum Conference (1992), states:

> The school and university curriculum needs to be transformed so that it will help students to view concepts, issues, and problems from diverse ethnic, cultural, and gender perspectives. An important goal of education in a democratic society should be to free all students of their cultural encapsulation and to help reform society so that citizens from all groups can freely participate.

Interpersonal and communication competence. In our increasingly interdependent world, the abilities to communicate clearly and relate well interpersonally are key areas of schooling. Language development needs to be nurtured throughout the school day and across the curriculum by all teachers. Every teacher, whether his or her subject area is mathematics, science, social studies, or the arts, is a teacher of language. Language is the personal tool that each student uses to access, ponder, create, and portray information so that it truly exemplifies knowledge. In addition, the business community is calling for workers who can communicate clearly and relate well interpersonally across cultures. As the workforce becomes more culturally diverse, the ability to communicate clearly in verbal, visual, and written forms becomes increasingly important.

Technological competence. The use of technology to access information, to improve communication, and to allow for creative lessons and expression must be an integral part of schooling. As well as providing access to, and sorting large bodies of, information, technology allows for a multimedia approach for the display of knowledge. As such, it becomes a "thinking tool" as students manipulate, create, and report information. When used appropriately, technology assists students in taking control of their learning. The interactive aspect of technology motivates the mind as students direct and choreograph the display of learning.

Aesthetic competence. Learning is enhanced and life is more greatly appreciated when a person has aesthetic competence. The geniuses of our world make use of visualization and artistic renderings to form and convey their ideas. Darwin drew trees to process his thoughts on the origins of humans; Einstein visualized a ride on a beam of light when working on the theory of relativity.

Aesthetic sight aids insight. The creative side of the mind's eye provides a window of unlimited discoveries. Whether visualization and metaphor are used to deepen understanding of existing forms, or to create new forms, they enhance the landscape of thought.

Outcomes Versus Objectives

We have made the transition (some districts better than others) from a focus on "student learning objectives" to a focus on "student process outcomes." What is the difference? It has been interesting to watch districts grapple with the transition in terminology and philosophy.

Student learning objectives—SLOs—once filled the pages of curriculum guides that were to be the teaching bibles for everything an educated student should know. Curriculum specialists throughout the country took pride during the 1970s and 1980s in being able to identify the correct level of specificity for General Instructional Objectives versus Specific Instructional Objectives. I was the Verb Queen of Montana, leading committee after committee in the development of big books of content objectives—with a few affective objectives thrown in here and there. The books looked impressive! But there were problems:

- Teachers did not see them as helpful, and the books were usually nestled among dust balls in cluttered closets.
- The guides specified a verb for teachers to use with each piece of information to be learned—as if there were only one correct verb (process) to be used.
- As the amount of information kept expanding in each subject area, the books of objectives kept getting larger and more impossible to incorporate into the learning plan.
- Textbook publishers began putting student learning objectives into the teachers' manuals, and the committee work became a lesson in redundancy.

TRADITIONAL OBJECTIVES

- Objectives are measurable and are usually assessed through paper-and-pencil multiple choice or short answer tests.

- Objectives are what you want students to know; the primary focus is on the mastery of content information.

- Some objectives are written to engage the affective areas such as the following: "Select reading materials to indicate an enjoyment of reading."

- General Instructional Objectives contain a process verb, such as "Understand Numbers and Numeration"; but the student assessment of "understanding" is based on specific lower level objectives, such as "Identify examples of the Commutative Law," rather than on a demonstrated depth of understanding through the application of knowledge in meaningful contexts.

Figure 2.2. Traditional Objectives

– When it was suggested that perhaps the publisher's objectives would suffice, educational rhetoric prevailed: "Oh, no . . . we can't let a textbook dictate our curriculum," and the redundancy continued.

With the realization in the mid-1980s that memorizing growing lists of content objectives was not achieving the outcomes needed for a rapidly changing society, the focus for curriculum and instruction changed dramatically. Figures 2.2 and 2.3 examine some of the basic questions and issues surrounding this shift in focus.

What is the difference between traditional objectives and today's process outcomes? Traditional objectives focus on a specific piece of content or an identified skill. Process outcomes are complex demonstrations of individual, and personal, development. Traditional objectives lead to direct transfer of learning; process outcomes facilitate elevated, or higher level, transfer of learning. Direct and elevated transfer of learning are defined in greater detail in Chapter 3.

OUTCOMES

- Outcomes are what you want students to be able to do, and are applied across the critical content of what you want students to know.

- Outcomes are measured developmentally through performance assessments.

- Outcomes focus on personal process abilities or competencies, such as the ability to think or communicate.

- Outcomes develop the skills for "lifelong learning."

- Outcomes rely more on individual measures of achievement rather than on standardized measures.

- Successful performance on outcomes is dependent on a context of developmentally appropriate content.

- State and district frameworks usually specify one or two broad content outcomes in addition to four or five process outcomes.

Figure 2.3. Outcomes

Why change from objectives to outcomes? The 21st century requires work and living skills that are highly sophisticated compared with the work and living skills required in past history. Advances in technology, the uses of technology in the workplace, the increasing interdependence of our world in social, economic, and political spheres, and the general complexity of life today call for a better balance between content expertise and personal performance. The SCANS competencies and trend data show clearly the changing life needs that are affecting the way we do business in the schools.

What does the shift from objectives to outcomes mean for curriculum and instruction? The growing emphasis on process outcomes means that curriculum and instruction will continue to become more focused and relevant. Curriculum will be organized around major concepts, themes, problems, and issues that will require the use of increasingly sophisticated cognitive and language process skills. Instruction will employ many different teaching strategies from direct, didactic lecture to facilitation of individual and group learning experiences. The goal of instruction will not be memorization of isolated facts but quality of performance and evidence of analytical and creative thinking related to critical content. Technology will play an increasingly important role as a tool for managing information and displaying knowledge.

How is content being addressed in the new outcomes paradigm? There are a variety of approaches being advocated to address content with an outcomes-driven curriculum. At one extreme are the people who value personal process skills so highly that they feel the identification and articulation of specified content is of little importance.

Another extreme, which is more traditional, is that students must rigorously study and learn foundational content in elementary and secondary schools and then concentrate on developing the process skills to sophisticated levels in postsecondary schools.

A third approach asserts that content and process must always appear together because they are only effective when they are joined. This belief system looks at both content and process as jointly increasing in complexity through the grades. The state and national outcome frameworks are often based on this belief.

The approach advocated in this book views content and process as two different strands in instructional planning. Even though content and process both appear in greater complexity and sophistication as students progress through the grades, there must be a plan for articulating the development separately. The reason for this is that content and process are not defined and articulated in the same manner. Nor are they taught or assessed in the same manner.

Later in this chapter, I will share the Federal Way, Washington, model for aligning course and grade-level performances with district performance outcomes. When the graduating standard is set as a Program Outcome, it is a relatively easy task to design the grade-level developmental performances that lead to the target. Sampling assessments of the performance outcomes measure progress through the grades.

Outcomes at the National Level

The President's Goals and the America 2000 legislation outline the following ideals, presented in abbreviated form, for our national educational system:

- All children will begin school ready to learn.
- There will be a 90% graduation rate in the United States.
- The United States will be the first in the world in mathematics and science achievement.
- Every adult will be literate and able to compete in the workforce.
- We will have safe, disciplined, drug-free schools.

As a result of this focus, national leadership organizations in the various subject areas are developing content and process standards as well as performance assessments for the various disciplines. The National Council of Teachers of Mathematics was the first to deliver their framework for what students should know and be able to do in the field of mathematics for the 21st century. Since that time the other disciplines have been working to produce guiding documents geared toward the development of higher order thinking and performance. As a curriculum specialist, I find the national and state curriculum frameworks helpful in portraying the best thinking and research of the day related to the content and process skills for the different disciplines. I fear assessment overkill, however, and cautiously await the application and implementation plans.

I attended some of the national standards hearings. The standards for social studies (Figure 2.4) provide an integrative approach to curriculum based on major concepts such as *Culture; Citizenship; Time, Continuity; Change;* and *Global Connections.* My experience supports the social studies perspective that elementary and secondary school students retain more historical knowledge when it is presented in the context of passionate perspectives and the experiences of people and cultures, framed by conceptually based themes

Culture Middle Grades	Social studies programs should include experiences that provide for the study of *culture and cultural diversity*, so that the learner can:

Performance Expectations:

a. compare commonalities and differences in the ways groups, societies, and cultures meet human needs and concerns;

b. explain how information and experiences may be interpreted by people from diverse cultural perspectives and frames of reference;

c. explain and give examples of how language, literature, the arts, architecture, and other artifacts, traditions, beliefs, values, and behaviors contribute to the development and transmission of culture;

d. explain why individuals and groups respond differently to their physical and social environments and/or changes to them on the basis of shared assumptions, values and beliefs;

e. articulate the implications of cultural diversity, as well as cohesion, within and across groups.

Figure 2.4. National Social Studies Standards
SOURCE: National Council for the Social Studies; used by permission.

through time. I believe this approach helps students develop a systems view of events, so that they can understand current day examples of a concept from the past lessons of history.

In developing the national Geography Assessment Framework, the Council of Chief State School Officers with the National Council for Geographic Education (1994) also based their framework on major concepts and organizing themes in that field. The concepts of *Scale, Change, Diversity, Models,* and *Systems* are developed through the five themes of location, place, human/environment interaction, movement, and regions.

Concept-based frameworks are workable formats for schools. The performance indicators for each of the concepts are developed through broad topics of critical content. The frameworks are general enough to allow teachers the flexibility and latitude to design the curricular plan. Overprescription of curricular content at the national or state levels robs teachers of the opportunity to thoughtfully plan what and why they are teaching. We want to encourage thinking teachers who have the desire and initiative to plan and design curricular and instructional programs. Thinking teachers inspire thinking students.

Outcomes at the State Level

How are today's state curriculum frameworks presenting the process outcomes and identified critical content? States around the country are identifying broad graduation outcomes that are process based. They may also include one or two graduation outcomes that call for student understanding and application of the major concepts and principles in the academic subject areas such as science and mathematics. These outcomes are defined by representative state committees composed of parents, business leaders, teachers, administrators, university professors, and, in some states, students. Figure 2.5 shows a representation of the kinds of outcomes found in state frameworks.

State-level subject area committees, again with wide representation, then define the critical content in broad terms. A sample representation showing how critical content is defined at the state level is shown in Figure 2.6. These subject-specific frameworks provide "benchmark indicators" showing what students should developmentally know and be able to do at the various grade level groupings, such as K-2, 3-5, 6-8, and 9-12.

The benchmark **indicators** incorporate process skills aligned to the graduating outcomes and content topics that fall under the organizing ideas outlined in the state or district framework. It is important to recognize that the benchmark performances that combine content and process skills are for the purposes of assessment. They are not intended to provide an articulated content curriculum.

In the mathematics example in Fugure 2.6, the content outcome, "develop concepts," and the process outcome, "communicate number relationships," are carried out through the activity of problem

---

STATE GOAL EXAMPLES

There are broad state outcomes, which are sometimes called "goals."

1. Communicate effectively through verbal, written, and visual forms.

2. Use critical and creative thinking ability to solve problems and to create knowledge.

3. Know and apply the key concepts and principles of science, mathematics, and other academic subjects.

Figure 2.5. State Goal Examples

solving in group activities. The concept-based, content outcome and the student processes of problem solving and communication are aligned with state goals 2 and 3 shown in Figure 2.5. The performance assessments must measure both the content and the process-based outcomes. Chapter 5 on assessment will give specific examples related to content/process assessment.

Designing Effective State Curricular Frameworks

State standards and assessments can be very helpful to districts, but they must be workable and usable for the classroom teacher. Once they are developed, the state has an obligation to see that districts receive clear direction and training on how to use the frameworks as they are aligned with the local curriculum. Curriculum developers for state frameworks need to ask the following questions:

- Has the issue of *time* been considered in the grand design of the frameworks?

  - Time for teacher training?
  - Time for design of district-level curriculum and instruction?

STATE SUBJECT AREA OUTCOMES

Separate subject area outcomes are developed at the state level by broad-based committees. These outcomes align with the state goals and national subject area frameworks and often provide the rationale for the activity (in order to . . .).

Mathematics Example:
Apply problem-solving strategies in group activities in order to . . .

• develop concepts of fractions, decimals, integers, and percents;
• communicate number relationships

Figure 2.6. State Subject Area Outcomes

- – Time for teachers and administrators to dialogue about the critical issues surrounding performance-based teaching and learning?
- – Time for teaching the mandated curricula?
- – Time for carrying out the performance-based assessments?
- – Time for evaluating and revising the frameworks prior to statewide implementation?

- • Have the developers of state frameworks sought initial and ongoing input from multiple sources and perspectives in the planning and design processes?
- • Has a **multidisciplinary** design team at the state level developed a common format for subject area frameworks so that teachers will be able to interpret them easily?
- • Do the frameworks explain clearly the shift in emphasis from a fact-based to a performance-based system of instruction and assessment? Do they tell why the emphasis has shifted?
- • Are the expectations for teachers as facilitators of educational change clearly spelled out?
- • Do the subject area frameworks provide flexibility to the districts in *how* they will meet the process and concept-based outcomes?
- • Are the frameworks clear in their layout?

- Are processes and concepts clearly identified as such to alert teachers to the developmental and content-based aspects of teaching and learning?
- Is the reason for the assessment performance stated—or do the activities appear to be for their own sake?
- Have we asked the critical questions related to what we hope to achieve as a result of the frameworks?
  - Do we want to develop only process skills to sophisticated levels?
  - Or do we also want to make certain that students have applied higher level thinking to go beyond memorization to deeper understanding of significant issues?

I value frameworks that address the process outcomes as developmental skills and address the content as essential learnings related to the major underlying concepts. The frameworks should be clear and to the point, and of similar format.

State curriculum frameworks need to address the key questions of development and implementation to realize the benefit for students. The issues of *framework design* across subjects; *time* for dialogue, curriculum writing, training, and teaching; and a *critical analysis* of instruction and student learning are basic to successful restructuring efforts.

Figure 2.7, an excerpt from a traditional music education state Framework, shows the Goals and General Objectives from a strand of Music Education. Skill-based objectives are related to the organizing concepts. The skill-based objectives are isolated, lower-level activities which require little personal creativity. I have provided a rewrite in Figure 2.8, which shows how the language and expectations change when an outcomes focus is used.

The goals and objectives from Figure 2.7 were combined to state the *what* and *why* of the outcome. The *how* is written at the district or classroom level unless a state writes detailed frameworks. The how is written most easily with the lead-in "... *by* ... " followed by the performance, as shown in Figure 2.8.

The grade-level performances identify processes that can be assessed developmentally, such as "discriminating sounds," but there

---

Traditional State Curriculum Framework
Music Education—Sample

Goals:

To increase aural awareness
To show musical enjoyment and participation
To understand the structure and form of music

Objectives: Students will . . .

- demonstrate an understanding of the production and modification of sound
- demonstrate and understanding of music concepts
- demonstrate an understanding of the form and function of music

Topics	Skill-based Objectives	
	Grade K-3	Grade 6-8
High/Low Notes	Identify high/low pitched sounds	Apply musical terms to pitch direction
	Recognize major/minor tonal qualities	Match voice and instrumental pitches
Rhythm	Recognize a change in rhythm	Identify a syncopated rhythm
Sound Modification		
Scales		

Figure 2.7. Traditional Curriculum Framework—Sample

is no way to know, from the process assessment alone, what generalizations or transferable lessons the student derived from the concept-based examples.

Because curriculum frameworks can often be used as tools to help teachers learn new skills, I would like to see a column added after each grade grouping that lists some of the key generalizations that students might derive from their learning experiences.

For example, two generalizations related to the grade groupings in Figure 2.8 are as follows:

Rewrite of Traditional State Framework
Music Education—Sample

Program Outcomes

1. Analyze the production and modification of sound
   in order to increase aural awareness . . .
2. Evaluate the form and function of music in order
   to apply appropriate concepts and principles . . .
3. Integrate the concepts, or elements, of music in order
   to be musically responsive, involved, and discriminating . . .

Concepts	Outcome Performances	
	Grades K-2	**Grades 6-8/7-9**
Pitch	. . . by . . .	. . . by . . .
	(1) discriminating and producing high/low pitched sounds;	(1) reading melodic patterns, and
		(3) creating a personal melody with
Rhythm	(2) using a drum to repeat a sample rhythm; then creating a new rhythm	varying pitch.
Harmony		
Form		
Tempo		

Figure 2.8. Outcomes-Driven Curriculum Framework—Sample

- K-2: Pitch affects sound.
- 6-9: Pitch is integral to harmony.

These examples are really *essential learnings.* They synthesize the lessons provided by representative examples. Generalizations require that students think at higher levels as they derive conceptual understanding that can be transferred to new examples. I fear this step has been left out of traditional curriculum designs for many years. Perhaps it was our love affair with easily scored questions that capped our thinking. Or perhaps it was a prevalent view that a fund of information equals intelligence.

The two frameworks shared in Figures 2.7 and 2.8 are similar in many ways, but the differences are significant. The traditional framework organizes the skill-based objectives by "topics." When the content is instead identified as major concepts, the instructor has a clear focus for the content topics that will be addressed in instruction. If teachers know the concepts they are teaching to, then the content can be defined as related critical topics. Because music is both a skill and a concept-based discipline, the district-level framework must speak to both skill development and concept attainment. Mathematics is also a skill-based and concept-based discipline.

The traditional framework has identified the basic skill objectives that teachers are expected to cover. The rewritten example gives only an expected performance at the state level and leaves the specific skills to be articulated at the district or school level.

Hybrid frameworks of old and new paradigms will continue to evolve toward a clearer vision of outcomes-driven frameworks for curriculum. Whatever the level of development, the designers have an obligation to convey clearly the format and appropriate use of these documents.

Outcomes at the District Level

School districts from Portland to Philadelphia are developing graduating student outcomes that are aligned with state outcomes. In most cases, the district outcomes are the result of a comprehensive committee process that looks at future trends, the needs of the local community, and the beliefs about what students should know and be able to do by the time they graduate. The committees are composed of parents and other community members, teachers, administrators, business people, and often students. Figure 2.9 provides a sample of district-level outcomes from Federal Way, Washington. The bullets identify the indicators, or attributes, of expected performance.

Districts grapple with the articulation and degree of emphasis to place on content as the shift in focus to process development continues.

When districts with process-based student outcomes say they are aligning their content curricula with their outcomes, they are misinformed. *Content does not align with process outcomes. Content aligns with concepts and content outcomes; process skills align with process outcomes.* Process skills are *applied* to content and form an interactive and

District Outcomes have 5-8 broad statements that are similar in wording to state goals. Each of the district Outcomes is defined further through specific performance indicators. These outcomes and performance indicators are useful to curriculum committees as they design subject area outcomes and the related design-down performance activities.

District Outcomes

1. Demonstrate competence in diverse forms of communication.
   - Use a variety of oral and written language forms
   - Apply technology to convey

2. Use thinking and reasoning strategies in order to solve problems and make decisions.
   - Recognize and clearly articulate problems
   - Select appropriate problem-solving strategies . . .

Figure 2.9 Sample District Outcomes
SOURCE: Federal Way Public Schools, Federal Way, Washington; used by permission.

supportive relationship. And students *use* process to manipulate content and evoke meaning.

It is true that both content and process become more cognitively sophisticated as students progress through the grades. But we must still consider the articulation of process and the articulation of content separately. They are assessed and aligned in totally different ways. We can develop a **rubric** that covers the measurement of both when they are brought into an interactive relationship. But if we present them only in an interactive relationship in district curriculum frameworks, we could easily miss critical concepts and content. We may also limit the use of process across the content fields by doing the linking at the district level.

The Student Outcomes for the Federal Way, Washington, Public Schools are given in Figure 2.10, followed by a sample of the performance indicators for higher level thinking related to District Outcome 1 (Figure 2.11). You will notice that the Federal Way Student Outcomes do not include a content outcome. These outcomes were developed five years ago when the focus was on process development. Districts are now returning to include a content outcome to have an anchor for aligning the content curriculum.

The following outcomes are based on the Federal Way Public Schools commitment to provide a comprehensive education that blends academic proficiency in areas of study such as language arts, mathematics, science, and social studies with the attitudes, values, and behaviors that are critical for success.

Future Trends	Outcome
1. Our complex world requires a high level of critical and creative thinking, decision-making, and problem-solving skills.	Students apply a variety of thinking and reasoning strategies to identify problems, solve problems, and make thoughtful decisions.
2. Society demands a high level of verbal, written, and techno-logical communication skills. Furthermore, as the amount of information increases, students need to access and organize it in a meaningful way.	Students demonstrate proficiency in many forms of communication.
3. As our family, social, and socie-tal structures change, positive self-esteem, independent liv-ing skills, and the willingness to consider the needs of others become more essential.	Students demonstrate respect, concern, and caring for themselves and others.
4. Success and fulfillment in the home, community, and work-place require effective team-work, including the ability to lead and follow.	Students work successfully in a group as collaborative and cooperative members.
5. Moral and ethical issues become greater as society be-comes more complex, requir-ing the ability and willingness to make responsible decisions.	Students understand and take responsibility for their actions, decisions, and behaviors.

Figure 2.10. Student Outcomes, Federal Way Public Schools
SOURCE: Federal Way Public Schools, Federal Way, Washington; used by permission.

(Continued)

Future Trends	Outcome
6. An interdependent world needs people who participate in and contribute to their communities.	Students understand their responsibilities, rights, and opportunities for participating in the local and world community.
7. Our global marketplace and multicultural society require understanding and acceptance of diversity.	Students understand and appreciate their own and other cultures.
8. In a rapidly changing society, the quality of life, both personal and in the workplace, will depend on the ability to grow and learn.	Students demonstrate skills and attitudes that enable them to be lifelong learners.

Figure 2.10. (Continued)

Student Outcomes and Developmental Performance

Many school districts that have developed their student outcomes are now ready to define the developmental performances at each level of schooling and are looking for workable models.

An approach that has proven easy for teachers and administrators to work with is the Federal Way developmental performance model presented in Figure 2.12.

In the model shown in Figure 2.12, the District Student Outcomes are listed at the top of the page. A curriculum committee of approximately 25 kindergarten through grade-12 teachers in the targeted subject area work for a day to identify three "Program Outcomes" that are related to one or more of the District Student Outcomes. (A "Program" is a K-12 subject such as language arts.) The committee also writes the grade-level tasks, or performances, for each of the Program Outcomes.

Future Trends
Our complex world requires a high level of critical and creative thinking, decision-making, and problem-solving skills.

OUTCOME 1
Students apply a variety of thinking and reasoning strategies to identify problems, solve problems, and make thoughtful decisions.

Performance Indicators

- Recognize and clearly define problems.

- Select appropriate problem-solving strategies.

- Think critically and creatively.
  - Use metacognitive techniques (reflective thinking).

- Show proficiency with a variety of problem-solving tools, such as

  - computation   - communication skills
  - logic   - information processing
  - technology   - conceptual understanding
  - critical analysis   - scientific process

- Determine whether decisions should be made independently or collaboratively.

- When making decisions:
  - Take risks.   - Use relevant data.
  - Consider a variety of viewpoints. - Confer with others.
  - Consider multiple solutions.   - Use appropriate resources.
  - Analyze consequences.   - Select appropriate medium.

- Implement solutions, where appropriate, and evaluate effectiveness.

- Anticipate problems by analyzing past practices and predicting future developments.

Figure 2.11. Performance Indicators for District Outcome 1, Federal Way Public Schools
SOURCE: Federal Way Public Schools, Federal Way, Washington; used by permission.

Example of Program Outcome and Developmental Performances for Language Arts

Program Outcome:

"Analyze, interpret, synthesize and/or evaluate print and/or non-print materials to make informed decisions . . ."

Grade-Level Developmental Performances:

grade 12 . . . by comparing and contrasting two pieces of literature for a purpose

grade 8 . . . by using school and community resources to research a topic and by presenting information to an audience

grade 4 . . . by demonstrating the ability to self-reflect/evaluate one's work through speaking, writing, or performing

grade 2 . . . by comparing/contrasting and evaluating one or more literary elements from several versions of the same story and presenting findings to the class

---

Figure 2.12. Federal Way Public Schools Performance Outcomes
SOURCE: Federal Way Public Schools, Federal Way, Washington; used by permission.

In developing the language arts Program Outcomes, the committee members ask themselves, "In preparation for the 21st century, what is a high-level outcome that we would like our students to demonstrate by the time they graduate from high school?" The Program Outcome is written as an open-ended statement. The developmental performance task, for each grade level or grade band, completes the Program Outcome Statement.

Teachers working as teams of two or three at each grade level on the committee complete the Program Outcome Statement by writing a **developmentally appropriate** performance task for each grade level, or grade span, that would contribute to the graduating Program Outcome. "Developmentally appropriate" refers to the match between the task and the students' cognitive, social, or physical ability to perform the task successfully. The students are assessed with a set of criteria and a standard that allows for a developmental range of performance levels on the task. Each student's *progress* is measured against the identified standard, however. Individual progress is to be celebrated according to the amount of growth achieved.

The value of this model is that the performance tasks at the various grade levels are based on activities that teachers carry out every day with their students. Developing the assessments for these performance tasks is a natural extension of the teaching/learning cycle.

Why don't the above grade-level performances contain specific content? Because it is intended that teachers will focus on using the process outcomes with different pieces of literature or other appropriate content throughout the year. If the specific pieces of content were listed in the district model, it could shut down the use of the processes across the curriculum.

For districtwide data, program outcomes are assessed by sampling the students' abilities on performance tasks at the different grade levels using developmentally appropriate content. The assessment criteria and standard are clearly defined.

Why are there only three program outcomes per subject area in this model? Because too many program outcomes for the different subject areas will mean that the outcomes sit on the shelf. The reality of the classroom is that for formal assessment purposes, teachers can focus only on a limited number of process skills throughout a day or year.

As program outcomes and developmental performance charts are made for the separate subject areas, a district matrix is developed that verifies that all of the student outcomes are being addressed across the different subject areas. It is also important to note that teachers will draw from many process skills as they design student interactions with content.

The major purpose for specifying some of the process skills that are developed through instruction is to increase teacher awareness of the growing emphasis on *systematically* developing each student's process abilities and to provide identified content/process samples for district assessment purposes.

Districts may wish to consider "sample assessments" at the district level to provide the public with evidence of progress toward the district outcomes. In language arts, for example, the district might assess the developmental performance identified by the teachers at grades 2, 4, 6, 8, 10, and 12 and identify grade-appropriate content to carry out the assessment. Accompanying rubrics define the assessment criteria and standard for the sampling task.

I recommend using grade-level performance assessments such as those shown in Figure 2.13 for district-level sampling of student development for the following reasons:

- We need to share results from performance-based assessments with the public if we wish to broaden their view of assessment beyond the normative-referenced, standardized tests.
- To try and operate a full-scale performance-based assessment program from the district level would be impractical. Schools do not have the time and personnel to handle the paper load and results monitoring.
- The best performance assessment is continuous and occurs in the context of the daily classroom experience. The district-level sampling procedure can emphasize the importance of performance assessment, and show teachers some techniques for designing performance tasks, but should never try and replace ongoing classroom assessment.

Outcomes at the Classroom Level

A huge issue for teachers is how to interpolate the state and district outcomes and essential learnings into the instructional program. There are a number of understandings that teachers need to have to design an effective outcomes-driven program for students:

1. All state and district outcome frameworks have three components: the critical *concepts and principles* that students need to understand; the critical content usually found listed as topics, or essential learnings, that are related to the organizing concepts; and the *process skills* that will be measured developmentally.

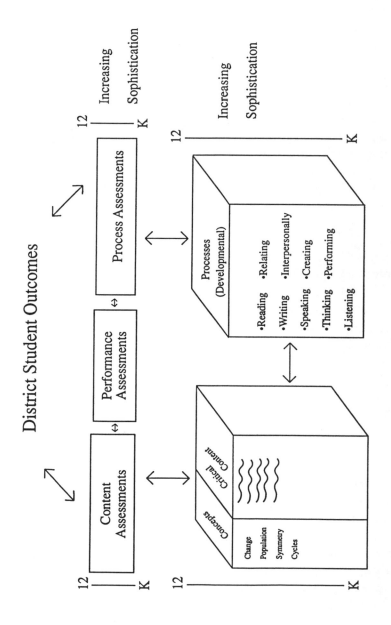

Figure 2.13. Relationship of Content to Process

57

2. Some of the frameworks clearly delineate these three compo- nents; others embed the concepts and critical content within the process statement, and it is necessary to ferret them out. A suggestion would be to pull out the concepts and related topics so as to see the expectations for the content strand of curricu- lum. Then, developmentally appropriate related topics for the grade level or course can be identified to determine if there are critical gaps in the content expectations.

3. The process outcomes identified in the frameworks must be measured developmentally and individually. Reading, writ- ing, speaking, listening, thinking, and all other process skills that develop internally in students must be assessed through performance-based measures, such as benchmark indicators, **portfolio** growth, and developmental writing or speaking assessments.

The Essential Relationship of Outcomes and Content

With the hoopla surrounding the development of process out- comes, the discussion of content has faded into the background, leaving many people to wonder, "Where did it go?" Earlier in this chapter, I told of the different positions concerning the emphasis that should be placed on both content and process in curriculum and instruction. Figure 2.13 shows the distinct, yet interdependent rela- tionship between content and process.

In Figure 2.13, process skills are aligned with program and district outcomes and are measured with performance assessments. Content is aligned with the major organizing concepts and leads to generali- zations, principles, and theories that are measured through perform- ance assessments. The content is aligned to the content-based pro- gram and district outcomes by way of the organizing concepts.

Critical to note is the fact that students use personal process skills to interact with content, which is inert and useless by itself. The interaction creates knowledge. In the following chapter, concepts are used to structure the fact-based curriculum.

SUMMARY

Technology, economic competitiveness, and increasing global interactions are shaping the direction of schooling in America. Curriculum and instruction are heavily weighted with innovation. In deciding how to proceed, teachers weigh society's needs against past teaching practices and their beliefs about teaching and learning. The job of educator has never been more challenging or complex.

Curriculum is no longer a simple matter of readin', writin', and 'rithmetic or memorizing facts for a multiple-choice test. Today, curriculum includes what students can do with content—how well they think, problem solve, and work as members of a team. Instruction goes beyond isolated memory drill to helping students synthesize information to gain a deeper understanding of the concepts and generalizations that will have lasting value as they structure knowledge and interpret their world.

The 21st century demands more of our educational system than the traditional focus on fact-based mastery. This outmoded curricular model, which makes increasingly futile attempts to race through textbooks packed with trivia, is doomed to failure.

The current trend to balance the essential and lasting learnings of critical content with student process, or performance outcomes, brings focus, relevance, and meaning to the educational program. We are concerned with the developing abilities of every child to handle vast amounts of information coming from many sources as they work with life-related problems, issues, and questions.

Extending Thought

1. How much influence should business have on school curricula?
2. Do you feel the concern of the business community about the skills of workers is legitimate?
3. Some liberal arts educators, such as history or literature teachers, say that we will lose the integrity of academic ideas if we let business dictate an integration of academic/vocational curricula. How would you respond?

4. How would you define the components of a balanced, "whole-child" curriculum?

5. What is the importance of the arts to a child's development?

6. How does the new definition of curriculum presented in this chapter represent current thought and practice?

7. Why are *outcomes* of more lasting value than *objectives* in the educational experience?

8. Why is it imperative that teaching and learning refocus to a higher cognitive plane in the classroom?

9. How does the role of the teacher change in a classroom focused on the attainment of process and content outcomes?

10. How does the role of the student change in an outcomes-based classroom?

11. How can you involve parents in the design and delivery of your curricular plan so that they understand and support the positive changes?

12. How can you work with extremist segments of the population so that you hear and value their positions yet weigh those beliefs with the majority views, the needs of society, and the foundational principles of democracy?

CHAPTER 3

Creating Concept-Based Curricula

We are caught in a curious blend of old content and new. Societal trends have foisted a pot of mulligan stew at the schoolhouse door. Curricula for AIDS, personal safety, and drugs and alcohol, developed with the best of intentions, threaten to drive teachers to the brink. Principals cringe to hear that they must ask teachers to toss in just "one more thing." This continual addition of ingredients, into the simmering curriculum stew, has created a crisis. We are losing sight of significant knowledge and ideas. They are drowning in the mix.

Process outcomes address the personal abilities that students will need for responding to the trends, but they do nothing to address the problems of subject area content. How do we make decisions on what content is most valuable to include in our limited school hours? And how do we ensure that meaningless content will be replaced?

- Kindergarten classes do "The Farm" and "The Circus." And maybe they should—but has anyone questioned whether these are the best topics for today's curriculum?
- Writing classes do creative writing, but how many schools teach technical writing—a critical skill for so many future jobs?
- Community organizations develop full curricula on specific topics to help educate future citizens to their cause. Fire, water,

energy, teeth, heart, fitness, smoking, personal development, safety, and recycling—all are socially valuable. But are we tossing together a curriculum of fragmented topics rather than a reasoned, coordinated, and articulated plan for learning?

- American history classes live in the past and race toward the future but often crash at the end of World War II. The dogged pursuit of a chronological compendium of events contributes to the loss of the big ideas—the lasting lessons of history.

Factual content is too often taught as an end in schooling. The *use* of content, the *applications* of content, and the *"so what?"* of content are curiously avoided in the traditional curriculum.

Traditional Curriculum

Teachers often rely on textbooks to tell them what to teach. Yet textbooks, because of their topical focus, fail to address the higher level, lasting ideas that can be applied to current and future trends.

For the last 100 years, the curriculum has been governed by discrete subject areas and topical organizers for content. There has been no differentiation between the subjects of science and social studies and the processes of reading and writing. All were treated as subjects of content and skills to be memorized. Figure 3.1 shows the traditional models of discrete subjects, topics, and content. The focus in traditional schooling has been on memorization of an increasing body of facts.

The problem with this model is that the information base in our world is challenging the best of microchips. School districts trying to keep up with this information explosion continue to publish bulging curriculum guides in quiet defiance of the pleas to "save a tree." These guides, which teachers soon forget they have, list hundreds of isolated student learning objectives. They usually tickle only the lowest cognitive levels and serve as fodder for a trivial pursuit intellect.

The effect of this lower level love affair with trivia is that we have lost sight of the higher level learnings. Kings, queens, and dates, the presidents and all their men: What significance do they hold for

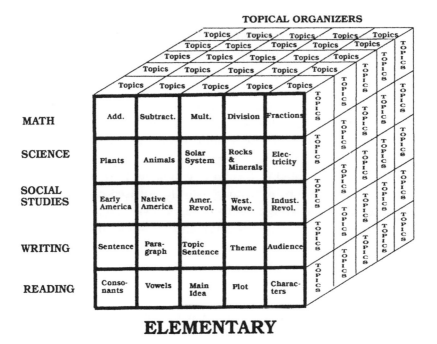

Figure 3.1. Traditional Model: Fact-Based Curricula

understanding our world and the human condition? Certainly, they hold little significance as isolated bits of stored memory. But as key historical players in life's drama, their social situations, actions, and reactions hold lessons for understanding the human condition today and for predicting the world of tomorrow.

There is a debate taking place between historians and social studies educators as to the best approach for teaching content. Both groups have developed a set of national standards for their discipline, and both integrate economics, politics, sociology, anthropology, and geography. The primary differences appear to be in the degree of emphasis placed on the chronological study of people and events in the various periods of time and on the perspectives of Western versus multicultural views.

There is value in the beliefs and aims of both the social studies and the history educators. But we will continue to lose the lessons of history if we do not figure out a more efficient method for engaging students in the study. The traditional method has been relying too heavily on didactic lecture, especially at the secondary and postsecondary levels. Yet the aims of historians, to develop historical knowledge and reasoning in students, are laudable. How can we meet these aims in a manner that will involve and motivate students? How can we help students use the lessons of history to evaluate current situations? How can we foster the development of citizens who will live and work in an interdependent world?

The model presented in this book will show how the events of history become lessons of history with the focused exploration of concepts, and their representative examples, viewed through time. Culture and change, trade, justice, law and order, and diversity/commonality provide rich contexts for focused, thematic units that allow the student to search for lasting knowledge.

Concept-Based Curriculum

Concepts are the foundational organizers for both integrated curriculum and for single-subject curriculum design. They serve as a bridge between subjects, topics, generalizations, and levels of thought.

Hilda Taba, a visionary educator of the 1950s and 1960s, saw the value of conceptual organizers for content. Her research on developing higher levels of thinking was funded through a Federal Department of Education Research Project that she completed in February 1966 at San Francisco State College. Today, more than ever before, we need to reexamine Taba's views and extend her work—because she provides a positive direction for increasing the intellectual functioning of students. Development of critical and creative thinking is essential for the 21st-century challenge.

Historical Perspective: Hilda Taba

Taba (1966) refers to concepts as "high level abstractions expressed in verbal cues and labels, e.g., interdependence, cultural change and causality" (p. 48). She knew that a person's understanding of a

Table 3.1. Graduated Examples of Force

Grade 4	Grade 8	Grade 12
General Science	Physical Science	Physics
Force as action/ reaction	Newton's Second Law of Momentum	Friction
Pulleys and force	Machines and gravity	Hydraulics
Gravity as a force	Pressure	Pneumatics
Reduction of force	Energy transfer	Torque
		Inclined plane
		Trajectory
		Force and planets

concept grows as he or she experiences increasingly complex, conceptual examples. In science, for example, a student might learn about the concept of force at grades 4, 8, and 12, but the topical examples would become more abstract and complex as the child progressed (Table 3.1).

Taba referred to "generalizations and principles" as the *main ideas* of the content under study. She differentiated generalizations from principles by stating that generalizations usually included qualifiers in their statements, such as in the following: "Conflict is *often* caused by misunderstanding." Taba proposed that content coverage could be focused and delimited by letting the main ideas, or generalizations, determine the direction and depth for instruction. She held that specific information should be sampled rather than covered (Taba, 1966, p. 49).

Another insightful Taba truism was the observation that learning has multiple objectives—the learning of content and the learning of increasingly sophisticated behaviors in thinking, attitudes, and skills—and these objectives call for different forms of instruction at different levels of complexity.

Taba's study consisted of an experimental research design using a trained group of 12 teachers and a control group of 12 untrained teachers. All of the elementary-grade teachers instructed students with a social studies curriculum that used topically based content as the vehicle for teaching to the major organizing concepts and main ideas.

The trained teachers received 10 days of intensive instruction on using the social studies curriculum as a tool for developing students' cognitive processing abilities. Trained teachers learned to sequence and pace instruction to allow for maximum student response. The concept formation strategy required students to identify what they were seeing, formulate groupings of items by common characteristics, and label and subsume like items under organizing concepts.

Taba found that the cognitive maps of the teacher were critical to facilitating the cognitive development of the child. By "cognitive map," Taba was referring to the levels of understanding related to the content under study as well as the nature of the thinking processes. The teacher's task of "protecting the student's creative and autonomous thinking," while at the same time reinforcing the logic of content, called for high sensitivity in the instructional setting (Taba, 1966, p. 60).

Taba's research found that students in the trained groups showed a greater number of thought units, which were also longer and more complex than the control groups. The trained students exhibited the convergence of low- and high-level thought units into logical generalizations (the main ideas) related to the content.

Though the greatest problem for the teachers was a feeling of pressure to cover the curriculum, test results demonstrated that the time spent on process teaching and learning did not impede strong achievement in learning the fact-based information (Taba, 1966).

Conceptual Organizers

A conceptually organized curriculum helps solve the problem of the overloaded curriculum. Concepts bring focus and depth to study and lead students to the higher level generalizations that have application to the life situations of today and tomorrow. It is important to clarify the issue of concepts in general before we return to their value in curriculum organization.

What is a concept? The highest level concept is a mental construct that is timeless, universal, and abstract. Though the examples of a concept may vary in content, the general descriptors of the concept will be the same. *Symmetry,* as a concept, has many different examples that vary in content, but the descriptors of symmetry in all of the examples are the same. Examples of symmetry can be found across disciplines, as in art, nature, or music. The descriptors, or characteristics, include *balance, exact correspondence of form,* and *equivalence.*

Concepts are a higher level of abstraction than facts in the structure of knowledge. They serve as cells for categorizing the factual examples. Conceptual understanding continues to grow more sophisticated as new examples fill each concept cell. Because higher level concepts are timeless, they may be studied through the ages. Because they are universal, their examples may be derived from cultures around the world.

It is common in educational circles today to hear the word *theme* being used for the ideas I am defining as *concepts.* The problem I have found with this practice is that the definition of *theme* is so loose that topics sometimes become confused with conceptual themes. This is a significant problem in integrated curriculum if the goal is higher level, integrated unit design. Topics will only bring you to the level of coordinated, multidisciplinary curriculum. This means that two or more subjects, or disciplines, are coordinated in instructional time and content to focus on a single topic. Integrated curriculum requires a conceptual as well as a topical focus.

Where do concepts fall in the structure of knowledge? Figure 3.2 illustrates the relationship of concepts to facts, generalizations, principles, and theories in the structure of knowledge. Traditionally in education we have spent the majority of our instructional time on the lowest cognitive level, the memorization of isolated facts.

I was surprised to realize, through my work in curriculum, the generally low level of cognitive education most of us have experienced in our educational paths. This has resulted largely from fact-based textbook and curriculum design. And we often teach as we were taught. Many educators today, however, know that students must be actively and mentally engaged in their learning. As a result, they are adjusting the learning experience. Unfortunately, many textbook materials continue to be structured with low cognitive expectations.

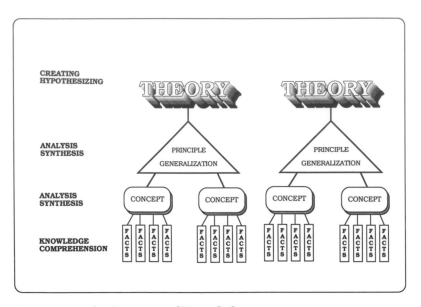

Figure 3.2. The Structure of Knowledge
SOURCE: Based on ideas of Hilda Taba.

Some people would argue that students cannot apply higher level thinking processes until they have a wealth of foundational knowledge. But that is not so. As a first-grade teacher, I enlisted creative and critical thinking from my students in the solution of problems. For example, using the concepts of *want* versus *need*, my students built new homes for our two imaginary pets, Chalk Mouse and Pencil Mouse. Chalk Mouse kept eating the teacher's chalk, and Pencil Mouse chewed on the pencils. They lost their homes in a natural disaster (the custodian accidentally disposed of them). The charge for students was to decide what a Chalk Mouse and Pencil Mouse would *need* and *want* in a home.

All students gathered their own materials for the project and went to work. They had chalk and pencils for them to eat, water to drink, ladders for their use in climbing up and down from desks, soft straw to lie on. Needless to say, this was the expression of critical and creative thinking at its finest. The room was buzzing with discussion of "need" versus "want." The critical point is that the students were responsible for solving the problem. I'm sorry to say that Chalk

Mouse turned to dust with the invention of the white board in classrooms.

Perhaps in the days of relatively unsophisticated technology and global isolationism, it was not as critical to think at high levels. But the game has changed. Global interdependence and sophisticated technologies require that we raise intellectual and academic standards in classrooms.

Figure 3.3 illustrates the value of elevated transfer of learning over à direct transfer of learning. Concepts elevate thinking to the level of abstraction, as shown by the stated examples. The alternative to an elevated transfer of learning is a direct transfer of learning, which has limited value in helping students achieve the high-level thought processes advocated by Robert Reich in Chapter 2. Both forms of transfer are important, however, in the overall learning plan.

What are some examples of the subject area organizing concepts? Teachers frequently want to know if there is a "master list of concepts in the sky" for each subject area. Except for the field of science, there are no formal lists at this time, but as we move toward national and state standards, it would be helpful to have national subject area organizations develop their lists of the most significant organizing concepts as frames for the critical content. Certainly, the dialogue among the professionals has started, but the task is not yet complete.

We need not wait, however. I have seen some of the most intense professional dialogue occur among subject area staff as they relate the content they teach to the organizing concepts. This process forces teachers to consider the most important ideas for instruction. Figure 3.4 shows some of the organizing concepts for six different subject areas. Please note that the concepts for literature are the traditional "themes" of literature. *Literature* is a conceptually based content subject, but *language arts* is a developmental process area.

In the previous examples, note the concepts that cut across disciplines. Because these concepts rise above the fact base and can be exemplified through multiple disciplines, they make excellent organizers for interdisciplinary, integrated curriculum—the focus of Chapter 4. The science concepts listed in the left-hand column were taken from a list first published by the Center for Unified Science in a journal newsletter, *Prism II* (Showalter, Cox, Holobinko, Thomson,

COGNITIVE BRIDGING

ELEVATED TRANSFER OF LEARNING

CONCEPT - BASED INSTRUCTION FOSTERS ELEVATED TRANSFER

A → DIRECT TRANSFER OF LEARNING → B

DIRECT TRANSFER (Point A → B):

(Formula and/or skill driven)

- Using mathematics computation to figure arithmetic problems in science, geography
- Applying word attack skills to reading
- Identifying the main idea of a paragraph after direct instruction on main idea
- Using formulas to mix solutions in chemistry
- Playing the notes of a musical composition

ELEVATED TRANSFER (Point A → B):

(Abstracting, Associating, Bridging)

- Using the concepts and principles of mathemtics to solve problems requiring abstract reasoning
- Analyzing, evaluating, and synthesizing information from different subject areas in order to more clearly understand a concept, problem or issue
- Comparing and relating the theme in a piece of literature to life situations dealing with universal concepts such as conflict, love, or family
- Deriving generalizations from the concepts of chemistry and using those generalizations to extend understanding
- Interpreting and conveying the mood of a musical composition

Figure 3.3. Transfer of Learning

Science	Social Studies	Literature
Cause/effect	Cause/effect	Cause/effect
Order	Order	Order
Organism	Patterns	Patterns
Population	Population	Character
System	System	Interconnections
Change	Change/culture	Change
Evolution	Evolution	Evolution
Cycle	Cycle	Cycle
Interaction	Interaction	Interaction
Energy matter	Perception	Perception
Equilibrium	Civilization	Intrigue
Field	Migration/	Passion
Force	immigration	Hate
Model	Interdependence	Love
Time/space	Diversity	Family
Theory	Conflict/cooperation	Conflict/cooperation
Fundamental	Innovation	
entities	Beliefs/values	
Replication		

Mathematics	Visual Art	Music
Number	Rhythm	Rhythm
Ratio	Line	Melody
Proportion	Color	Harmony
Scale	Value	Tone
Symmetry	Shape	Pitch
Probability	Texture	Texture
Pattern	Form	Form
Interaction	Space	Tempo
Cause/effect	Repetition	Dynamics
Order	Balance	Timbre
Quantification	Angle	Pattern
System	Perception	Perception
Theory	Position	
Field	Motion	
Gradient	Light	
Invariance		
Model		

Figure 3.4. Examples of Subject-Specific Concepts

& Oriedo, 1974). I suggested the concepts listed in the other subject areas to demonstrate that concepts can be cross-disciplinary, but disciplines are also framed by concepts that are unique to their field.

Identifying the major concepts is not as difficult as it first seems. If you were asked to name the major concepts for economics, *scarcity* and *supply and demand* would spring to mind. It is a matter of synthesizing topics with common characteristics with their organizing idea and running them through the following Concept Definition Test.

Concept Definition Test

Does the term you are considering as a higher level concept serve as a mental frame, or construct, for a class of examples? Does it meet the following criteria?

- Broad and abstract
- Represented by one or two words
- Universal in application
- Timeless—carries through the ages
- Represented by different examples that share common attributes

Example: Conflict, as a concept, has many different examples, but the examples share the characteristics of *opposing forces* and *friction*.

Let's try it. Which of the following are major organizing concepts? Apply each of the following terms to the Concept Definition Test:

Conflict	Persuasion
Family	Power
Culture	Revolution
Change	Model
Fitness	Dinosaurs
Human rights	Bears
China	Cooperation

How did you do? If you recognized that China, dinosaurs, and bears are *topics* that hold learning to the fact and activity base, then

Topical Organizers	Conceptual Organizers
Frame a set of isolated facts	Provide a mental schema for categorizing common examples
Maintain lower level thinking	Lead to higher levels of thinking
Hold learning to the fact or activity level	Aid in the development of higher order generalizations
Have short-term use—to cover an event, issue, or set of facts	Serve as a tool for processing life events
Increase the overload curriculum	Reduce the overload curriculum by framing the most salient, or critical, examples of the concepts

Figure 3.5. Topics Versus Concepts as Curriculum Organizers

you are correct. But remember that you can apply a concept to the study of a topic and you will shift learning to a higher cognitive plane. The concept of "extinction," attached to the topic of "dinosaurs," advances thinking to the conceptual level for younger students.

Why are concepts better than topics alone as curricular organizers? Figure 3.5 compares the value of concepts and topics as curricular organizers.

A New Look at Scope and Sequence

In the pages that follow, you will learn how to map critical content through the grades so that students develop increasing conceptual sophistication. You will see that facts are examples of their related concepts, and you will learn to design scope and sequence charts that foster the development of higher order thinking in students.

Traditional scope and sequence charts link facts to their topical organizers in page after page of low-level listings. In this book, you will discover a new look for scope and sequence charts. Instead of topical organizers for content, we will identify critical concepts for the different subject areas, teach you how to select the critical content for each concept through the grades, and, most important, teach you how to synthesize content to arrive at the key generalizations, or transferable lessons. You will learn how to avoid the trap of letting your activities in the classroom become *the end* of your lessons.

Higher order learnings are too often lost in classrooms. Fact-based or activity-based instruction fails to answer the relevancy question: "So what?" Teachers traditionally have not been trained to think through their lessons to the higher level learnings for students. When we study Native Americans, we learn where they lived and what foods they ate, but we have not learned to identify the *lessons* of the Native American experience over time. What if, instead, we structured the curriculum experience for students so that they could go on a search for knowledge related to Native American Culture and Change and arrive inductively at generalizations such as the ones that follow:

- A culture is severely disrupted when another culture dominates and intercedes.
- Cultures in contact influence each other in both positive and negative ways.
- Human-made laws may adversely affect a culture's traditional livelihood.

Unless we learn how to clearly identify the lessons of yesterday to help us solve the problems of today and tomorrow, we may be facilitating pointless content study.

The Tripartite Model for Curriculum

The complexity of curriculum design today is apparent as we move from a solely fact-based model to a **tripartite** model of curriculum. Figure 3.6 shows the usefulness of the tripartite model for single subject area curriculum design as well as for the Integrated Curriculum Model that will be described in Chapter 4.

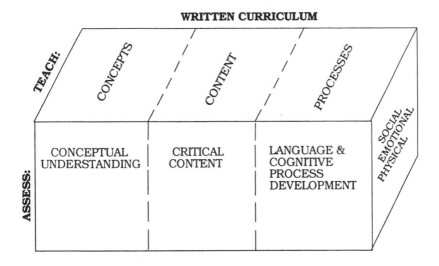

Figure 3.6. The Tripartite Curriculum Model

In the traditional model of curriculum, the focus is on the content. Content is organized by topics and, as the world information base expands, more topics are added to the bulging curriculum. We lack a rational plan for reducing content, and teaching becomes a skim of surface information.

In the model shown in Figure 3.6, content is organized conceptually rather than topically. This allows for a rational reduction in content because you can reduce the number of examples of a concept. If you are teaching about the concept of *conflict,* you can choose the examples related to the **topical theme,** whether "Conflict in American History" or "Conflict in Interpersonal Relationships."

When you teach conceptually, the focus shifts from memorizing isolated facts to understanding the lasting generalizations and principles related to the organizing concept and the thematic topics. The aim is higher level thinking centered on significant issues, questions, and problems.

Figure 3.6 shows the balance between conceptual understanding, critical content knowledge, and personal process development. If we are to increase the development of conceptual understanding and personal process skill, then we must make more time in the school day. This can only be accomplished by systematically reducing and focusing the content load.

The Outcomes movement that is developing on the American educational scene today addresses the three components of the tripartite model—concepts, content, and process—as essential to a comprehensive curriculum design. The emphasis placed on each component, or the balance of the three parts, depends on the form of outcomes curriculum design that a school or district chooses to follow.

The move toward a more balanced curriculum of content and process is really a move toward greater depth in teaching and learning as well as a focus on higher level thinking. If we want all children to be successful in developing the higher order skills outlined in district outcomes across the country, then we will move from topically based to concept-based curricula, from lower order to higher order process skills, and from meaningless to meaningful activities in the learning experience.

How can curriculum developers and committees organize content related to the major concepts? Content can be efficiently organized by relating the salient and critical topics of each major subject area to their organizing concepts. A simple format is the matrix. Figures 3.7, 3.8, 3.9, and 3.10 show examples from K-6 science curriculum and high school chemistry, economics, and world history curricula. These examples were developed by teachers in the Federal Way, Washington, Public Schools.

In the examples for K-6 science and chemistry, note that the concepts are repeated, but the related topics become more specialized and sophisticated as the student progresses through the grades. This format for organizing content allows for meaningful K-12 content articulation and ensures developing conceptual understanding. A concept-content matrix also allows the teacher to visually assess the "content load" of the course. If there are too many topics to

(text continues on page 82)

	KINDERGARTEN		1ST GRADE	
C O N C E P T U N I T S	**CAUSE/EFFECT** •Plant growth •Action/reaction •Color mixing •Movement •Sound pitches •Cause/effect in nature •Causes/effect of wind	**CHANGE** •Physical changes •Predicting changes •Recognizing changes •Body changes •Change as inevitable •Positive and negative changes •Observing changes •Creating change •Environmental change	**POPULATION** •Classifying populations •Family populations •Populations in nature •Animal populations (wild and domestic) •Zoo populations •Mealworm populations •Overpopulation •Endangered species population •Helpful populations	**ORDER** •Order by weight and length •Life cycle order •Order by amount of volume •Natural orders •Human -,imposed order •Creating an order •Alphabetical order •Sequencing events in order •Time orders •Interference of order

	2ND GRADE		3RD GRADE	
C O N C E P T U N I T S	**CYCLES** •Butterfly cycle •Mealworm cycle •Calendar cycles •Water cycles •Plant life cycles •Population cycles •Seasonal cycles •Recycle •Human impact on cycles	**SYSTEM** •Open and closed systems •Aquariums as a system •Circulatory system •Subsystems •Ecosystems •Fitness systems •School systems •Transportation systems •Solar system	**ENERGY MATTER** •Characteristics of matter •Characteristics of energy •Conservation of energy •Conservation of matter •Energy causes matter to change form •Identifying examples of energy and matter •Energy causes movement in matter •Identify the importance of energy/matter	**INTERACTION** •Change is evidence of interaction •Interaction between inanimate objects •Identifying interactions •Family interactions •Interactions between animate and inanimate objects •Humans can interact with inanimate objects •Man's interactions with his environment

	4TH GRADE		5TH GRADE	
C O N C E P T U N I T S	**SYMMETRY** •Symmetry in crystals •Importance of symmetry in flight •Symmetry in the plant world •Symmetry in the animal world •Symmetry in magnetism •Mirror images and symmetry •Creating symmetry •Lines of symmetry	**FORCE** •Force as action/reaction •Force and distance •Pulleys and force •Inclined planes •Force and resistance •Gravity as a force •Reduction of force •Force and pressure •Forces in our environment	**EQUILIBRIUM** •Weight and balance •Center of gravity and equilibrium •Factors that affect equilibrium •Molecular balance •Limiting factors •Balance of nature •Examples of equilibrium •Vocations that use the tools of equilibrium •Equilibrium and humans	**MODEL AND REMODEL** •Uses of scientific models •Characteristics of a model •Developing a scientific model •Testing a model •Using data to develop and change a model •Galaxies as a model •Model as an "idea"

	6TH GRADE	
C O N C E P T U N I T S	**ORGANISM** •Attributes of an organism •Fungi as organisms •Growing organisms •Distinguishing between living and nonliving •Classifying organisms •Recording organisms •Microscopic organisms •Environmental factors that affect organisms	**POPULATION** •Identifying populations •Classifying populations •Limiting factors of populations •Ecosystems •Competition for resources •Sampling populations •Predator/prey •Graphing populations •Environmental effects on populations

Figure 3.7. Elementary Science Kits Excerpt
SOURCE: Federal Way Public Schools, Federal Way, Washington; used by permission.

CONTENT STRANDS

CONCEPT	PROCESSES AND METHODS	ENERGY/THERMODYNAMICS	ATOMIC ENERGY	BONDING	MATTER	KINETIC THEORY	REACTIONS
Cause and effect	-controlled experimentation -safety	-entropy activation & potential energy	-significance of electron configuration -periodicity	-attachment between atoms		-heat & temperature -factors affecting reaction rate	-ionic reactions -molecular reactions
Change	-dimensional analysis	-conversion of energy -phase changes -entropy			-physical change -chemical change	-phase changes	-stoichiometry -oxidation reduction reactions
Energy matter	-naming compounds	-forms of energy	-light emission -absorption -ionization	-bond energy	-varieties of matter -physical or chemical properties	-heat & temperature -phase changes -enthalpy -entropy	-energy and chemical reactions
Equilibrium	-chemical formulas -solutions	-phase changes			-conservation of matter -conservation of atoms	-phase changes	-Le Chatelier principle
Fundamental entities	-mole		-atoms -molecules -electron -proton -neutron	-electrical interaction	-mole		-balancing equations -mole, -ph scale

Interaction		–ionization		–ionic bonds –covalent bonds –hydrogen bonds –polar bonds	–solubility –colligative properties	–factors affecting reaction rate	–limiting reaction –acid/base reaction
Model	–problem solving		–Dalton model –Thomson model –Bohr model –Quantum model –Charge cloud –Electron configuration	–VSEPR model –Lewis structure	–conservation of mass	–gas laws –collision theory –Hess's law	–collision theory –acid/base reaction
Probability	–percent error		–electron distribution –energy levels				
Quantification	–percent composition –graphing SI units –significant figure precision –concentrations of solutions	–scientific notation –measurement heat	–atomic weight –mass		–mole –percent composition		–stoichiometry

Figure 3.8. Chemistry: Concepts and Critical Content Matrix, Federal Way Public Schools
SOURCE: Federal Way Public Schools, Federal Way, Washington; used by permission.

CONCEPT	CONTENT	GENERALIZATIONS AND PRINCIPLES
Scarcity	Opportunity costs Choices personal national	The basic economic problem is scarcity. At any given time, each society has a given amount of labor, capital, and natural resources. People's wants for goods and services are greater than what can be produced. Because we cannot do, or have, everything all at once, we must make choices. Much of economics deals with analyzing how and why individuals, institutions, and societies make the choices they do.
Comparative systems	Command economy communism socialism Market economy business cycles capitalism	Every economic system institutionalizes the manner in which people decide what to produce, how to produce, and for whom to produce. Each economic system uses different means to answer these questions, based on its prevailing philosophical assumptions. Several economies rely more heavily on government and less on markets. The major ideas developed in this course will be to develop the concepts of the market economy as they are used in the United States.
Investments	Stocks Bonds Mutual funds Others	Investment capital comes from the people buying stocks and bonds from companies who use the needed capital to expand their production capacities and increase their productivity.
Supply and demand	Competition Utility Equilibrium	Markets are institutional arrangements that enable buyers and sellers to exchange goods and services. Changes in supply, or demand, or both, will cause changes in prices and in the amounts of goods or services produced and demanded. Competition thus forces the use of resources in an efficient manner.

Government regulation	Budget, debt Taxation Controls	Government guides the market in decision making by forcing it to respond to rules and regulations that are designed to achieve the objectives society has set and to answer its basic economic questions of what to produce, how to produce, and for whom to produce.
Monetary/fiscal	Federal reserve Government	Monetary policy attempts to regulate the general level of economic activity through the Federal Reserve System. It regulates the money supply by its activities. Congress and the president decide fiscal policy through taxing and spending policies.
Labor	History Unions Bargaining	The American labor movement exemplifies the working supply and demand in the job market. Unions are formed to maintain some control over jobs and lives and keep fairness in the workplace through collective bargaining.
International trade	Comparative advantage Balance of trade Restriction versus free trade	The concept of comparative advantage explains why nations benefit from specialization and trade with each other. Comparative advantage can allow goods and services for the least cost to be exchanged. However, this specialization might force a nation to become dependent upon others for basic needs. As a consequence, government often steps in with regulations designed to balance the flow of trade to ensure jobs and resources for itself.

Figure 3.9. Economics: Concepts and Critical Content Matrix, Federal Way Public Schools
SOURCE: Federal Way Public Schools, Federal Way, Washington; used by permission.

"cover," there will be less time for the student to develop the essential internal process skills for accessing, interpreting, and displaying knowledge. These are the essential skills for facilitating lifelong learning.

Two criteria are especially helpful in deciding which topics qualify as *critical content* to be included on the matrix:

- What do students need to know to be successful at the next level of learning? Multiplication, for example, is necessary prior knowledge for success with division.
- What do you, as a professional, feel that students need to know to understand the discipline? For example, in U.S. history, the American Revolution and the Civil War are two topics critical to an understanding of the subject.

The example from world history (Figure 3.10) shows the value of concept-based curriculum. The critical content serves as examples of historical concepts, and students have a frame of reference for deriving deeper understanding of the resulting generalizations and principles of history. It is the generalizations and principles that hold the lasting lessons of history. The facts support the generalizations.

How do we move from concept-content matrices to conceptual thematic teaching? To gain control of the burgeoning fact base, we can adapt the content matrices shown in the previous examples to conceptual, thematic charts that frame the design for learning.

In Federal Way, Washington, the eighth-grade U.S. history teachers felt that students were not retaining the information presented in the chronologically focused textbooks. They met for two summers in week-long institutes and wrote their own teaching units. These concept-based, thematic units incorporated the critical information of U.S. history. But they also engaged the students in learning activities that helped them view the different perspectives of people, related to concept-based events through time.

In their planning, the teachers developed a matrix of critical content (topics) related to four macroconcepts that they felt would cover the historical periods of the pre-Columbian era to Reconstruc-

Concept	Content	Generalizations/Principles
Inter-dependence	Interaction Cultural diffusion Isolation	Human beings develop interdependent relationships to meet needs and aid survival. This necessitates the formation of groups: societies, nations, and international organizations.
Continuity/ change	Innovation— science & technology Evolution Revolution Cause & effect Replication	History is a story of continuity and change. All societies promote continuity to survive, but a basic need to improve the conditions of living necessitates change.

Figure 3.10. World History Excerpt—Concepts and Critical Content
SOURCE: Adapted from Federal Way Public Schools Matrix, Federal Way, Washington.

tion. The four macroconcepts were "Culture and Change," "Conflict," "Justice," and "Trade."

At the next meeting they decided on three *topical themes* for each concept that would tell the story related to their critical content. Table 3.2 is an example of the concept-based "Culture and Change Unit." Note the three topical themes that were chosen to ground the content study and provide a focus for learning.

This matrix served as the planning document for the teachers as they wrote their units. Each macroconcept unit had two or three subunits governed by topical themes. The units themselves were activity driven and included such things as drama, music, art, literature, and debate. Though carried out in social studies classrooms, the units were interdisciplinary and could easily have been transformed into a cross-disciplinary team effort.

As part of the unit planning, the teachers thought through the content, relating it to the organizing concept, and identified some of the key generalizations that they expected students to derive. This step of thinking through to some of the resulting generalizations is essential for quality planning and teaching. Otherwise, we have no idea why we are teaching content. We need to look at the value of

Table 3.2. Grade 8 Social Studies: Scope and Sequence, Federal Way Public Schools

Themes	Unit I	Unit II		Unit III	
	Pre-Colombian to 1492	1492–1750	1750–1814	1814–1860	1860–1877
Native American Culture and Change	Theories of early migration	European culture in North America –adaptations –colonization	Development of unique American culture	Rise of nationalism Transportation	Slave/sharecropper (violent opposition to change)
Asian, European, and African Influences on American Culture and Change	Native American culture areas of North America	African migration Acculturation	Continuing separation from European cultures	Sectionalism/regionalism	Two emerging cultures (black/white)
The Development of Our Unique American Culture	Religion Migration	Religion –Puritans –Quakers Migration	Pioneer frontier spirit (French & Indian War cultural alliances) Land acquisition Religion Migration	Expansionism Westward Movement Gold Rush Mexican cession Texas (annexed) Chinese immigration Increasing European migration Indian removal east of Mississippi Rise of the machine –inventions Religion Migration	Rise of cities Religion Migration

SOURCE: Federal Way Public Schoolsl, Federal Way, Washington; used by permission.

generalizations in greater depth, for it is too often a missing component in traditional teaching and learning.

Generalizations

What are generalizations? Why are they so important for 21st-century education? Generalizations are the essential learnings, the "big ideas," the answer to the "so what?" of study. They synthesize the factual examples and summarize learning.

An excellent discussion of generalizations can be found in *Teaching Strategies for Ethnic Studies* by James Banks (1991). Banks differentiates between lower level, intermediate-level, and the highest, or universal-level generalizations that are related to a factual example:

> FACT: The Chinese immigrants who came to San Francisco in the 1800s established the *hui kuan.*
>
> *Lower-Level Generalization:* Chinese immigrants in America established various forms of social organizations.
>
> *Intermediate-Level Generalization:* All groups that have immigrated or migrated to the United States have established social organizations.
>
> *Universal-Level Generalization:* In all human societies, forms of social organizations emerge to satisfy the needs of individuals and groups. (Banks, 1991, pp. 43-45)

In this book, the focus is on universal generalizations—the essential learnings that have wide applicability through time and across cultures. These are the lasting lessons of history.

A few of the generalizations defined by the teachers in the "Culture and Change Unit" described previously included the following:

- Preexisting cultures influence migrating cultures.
- Interaction fosters cultural exchange.
- Cultural change is ongoing.
- Change causes conflict.
- Dominating cultures disrupt existing cultures.

Teachers do not usually tell students the generalizations; they lead students to inductively derive these transferable understandings. Students will also develop additional generalizations. It is important to ensure that their generalizations are supported in fact. At times students may make inaccurate generalizations, leaps of abstraction in their zeal to "know the answer." Teachers must think on their feet as they foster the development of higher level cognition through reasoning and critical thinking.

As I observe teachers over a period of time, I see growing sophistication in their ability to identify and state the essential learnings. When teachers first attempt to write generalizations, the thoughts are often simply stated, surface learnings. But as they learn to think beyond the obvious learnings to the deeper and lasting lessons, the generalizations show increasing sophistication. As teachers continue to develop personal capacities for synthesizing information, they learn to extend the thinking abilities of their students.

Some people feel that young children are not capable of abstracting to the level of generalizations. But children are capable of abstract thought and generalization when it is called for in the context of developmentally appropriate content.

As one example, a group of kindergarten and first-grade teachers in Richmond, Indiana, developed a unit around the concept of "Color" for their young students. The theme they chose was "The Value of Color in Our Rainbow World." They engaged students in many activities that demonstrated the theme, such as the following:

- Scarf drapings to decide as a group whether each child looked best in winter, spring, summer, or fall colors
- Environmental walks to note and appreciate the use of color for aesthetics as well as for safety
- Studies of color as a way to tell items apart

When asked how color helps us in our world, the children were able to generalize, with a little help on the lead-in: "Color—" ". . . makes us pretty," ". . . keeps us safe," ". . . tells things apart."

Generalizations are summaries of thought and answer the relevancy question, "What do I know as a result of my study?" Generalizations are higher level learnings that have transferability through time. They are applicable to all examples of the related concepts—both now and in the future.

Generalizations hold truth as long as they are supported by the examples. Banks explains that, even though a generalization is capable of being tested or verified, it can never be proven absolutely to be correct. Because of the complexity of human behavior, generalizations in the social and behavioral sciences are necessarily tentative and often contain qualifiers such as *sometimes* or *usually* (Banks, 1991). They are important, however, as higher level summaries of thought, which show conceptual relationships.

A Universal Generalization Defined

A generalization is defined formally as two or more concepts stated in a relationship. They are scientific statements that can be tested and verified with data (Banks, 1991, p. 42).

Universal generalizations have the same characteristics as a concept:

- Broad and abstract
- Universal in application
- Generally timeless—carry through the ages
- Represented by different examples, but the examples support the generalization

Universal generalizations, as they are written, use no past, past perfect, or present perfect tenses. To do so would set them in time as a fact. For example, "Poverty was a catalyst for migration" is past tense and may be a factual generalization related to a particular group, or groups, of people, but it is not a timeless, universal generalization, as stated.

Though generalizations are usually timeless, they are more susceptible to demise than concepts. Concepts remain timeless, but because generalizations are interdependent variables in a relationship, they may change over time with the alteration of either variable's circumstances. For example, a current generalization could be as follows: "A balanced diet ensures a healthy body." But if our diet becomes affected too heavily by pollutants, the generalization will not hold. Generalizations are helpful constructs for summarizing conceptual relationships, but their timeless validity must continually be verified through analysis of contemporary, factual examples.

Universal generalizations avoid proper and personal nouns. "Japanese trade affects the American economy" is a fact because it states the specific examples, Japanese and American. The universal and more timeless generalization is written, "Trade affects an economy." This statement can be supported through time, by numerous examples. Concepts and generalizations provide a framework for the articulation and coordination of curriculum in both single-grade and multiage schooling structures.

Multiage Classrooms and Concept-Based Curriculum

There is renewed interest in multiage classrooms and nongraded education. Multiage classrooms combine two or three grade levels to provide a broader age span for the learning environment. There are benefits from these arrangements as long as the teacher has a solid understanding of how to approach curriculum and instruction with the increased span of abilities and maturity levels.

One of the questions that arises most frequently is: How do we handle the multiple levels of curriculum within the multiage structure? Another example from Federal Way demonstrates the use of concepts, themes, and generalizations as an effective way to articulate the content curriculum in a multigrade or multiage school setting.

A dedicated group of 54 elementary teachers and librarians in Federal Way are involved in a major project to write an International Social Studies curriculum for the district's elementary program. Realizing our students will work and live in an increasingly multicultural, international context, the teachers developed a K-6 framework that addresses key concepts using examples from different cultural regions of the world.

Table 3.3 shows how the major social studies concept of "Diversity/ Commonality" is taught through *topical themes.* Examples of such themes are "Diversity and Commonality in Self and Family" in kindergarten and "Diversity/Commonality in Family and Neighborhood" and in "Neighborhood and Community" in grades 1 and 2. This model allows for developing sophistication in conceptual understanding as students progress from learning the generalizations related to "Diversity/Commonality in Families" in kindergarten through "Diversity/Commonality in in Our World" at grade 6. It is easy to see how the attachment of a conceptual focus to the traditional content takes thinking and learning to a higher level. The students participate in many activities to experience the concept and theme. Some of the generalizations that guide the learning activities for the concept of "Interdependence" include the following:

- Families work together to provide for needs and wants (K-1 grade levels).
- Nations work together to solve problems (pollution, arms race, and so on—grade 5).
- A nation's resources affect its dependence/interdependence ratio in the world economy (grades 5, 6).

Another interesting facet of the Federal Way model is the use of geographic *biomes* (world geographic regions having similar climate and vegetation) to identify other cultures for study. Each grade level chooses cultures from within a particular biome for in-depth study. The teachers reasoned that selecting cultures from different biomes allows students to learn how cultural groups interact with, and use, diverse environments for living. It also provides a representative sampling of cultures from around the world.

For multigrade classes, the use of major concepts in social studies as K-6 organizers allows teachers to use related topical themes each year. As long as the concept stays the same, different themes can focus the content across age levels or grade spans. Either teachers can have students working on different themes related to the concept in a classroom or they can do a different theme each year for the same concept.

Table 3.3. Social Studies Excerpt: K-6 Social Studies, Federal Way School District

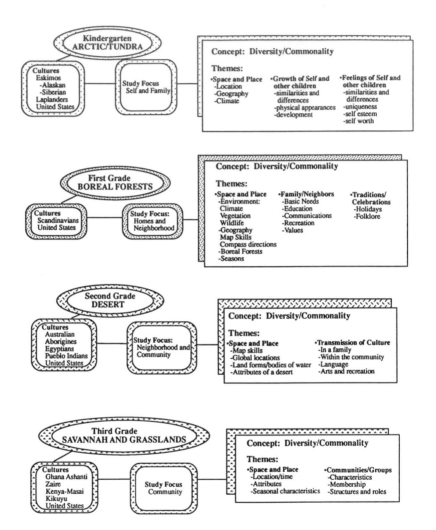

Table 3.3 Continued

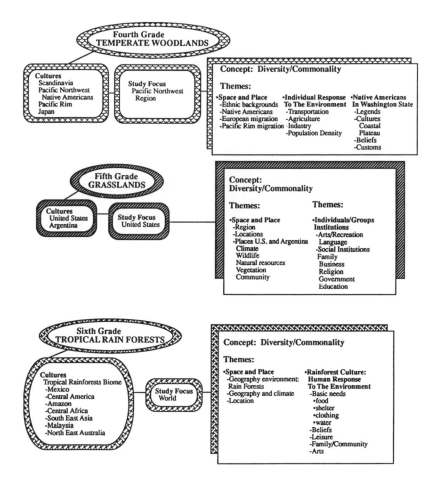

This social studies format allows for easy integration of curriculum as literature, art, music, drama, or other related subject area topics are brought into the design.

Chapter 4 proposes a general model for integrating curriculum that addresses the overloaded information base. This model focuses teaching and learning toward higher cognitive levels, integrates the study of subject area disciplines under a common concept, theme, problem, or issue, and differentiates between the developmental processes and content subjects.

The move toward integrated curriculum is progressing slowly as teachers and administrators learn as they go. It is important to move forward at a pace that allows for cognitive processing of "what works" and "what doesn't." One approach that does not work is to jump too quickly from single subject area curriculum designs into seamless, integrated curriculum. If we lose the structure of the separate disciplines, we run the risk of losing many critical concepts and skills and of destroying a coherent plan for knowledge development. We first need to start with the articulation of the critical concepts and content for each discipline and then work toward logically articulated, integrated curricula.

SUMMARY

The use of universal and lasting concepts to structure the massive amount of content, as we work with students, provides a rational plan for teaching to the essential learnings, or generalizations. Concept-based curriculum and instruction solves the problems of

- how to reduce the overloaded curriculum,
- how to articulate K-12 curriculum to develop higher level thinking and understanding, and
- how to plan curriculum for multiage classrooms and interdisciplinary instruction.

Concept-based curriculum design allows the teacher to control, rather than be controlled by, the subject matter and provides the flexibility to allow students to search for and construct knowledge.

Extending Thought

1. How does concept-based curriculum design reach beyond the memorization of isolated facts?

2. When students dialogue about issues at a conceptual level, they are debating a variety of perspectives. What are the ramifications for instruction? Teacher responsibilities?

3. How are topics used to develop conceptual understanding as students progress through the grades?

4. Why is a conceptual schema important as a framework for learning in today's world?

5. How can the study of historical examples of concepts through time, and resulting generalizations, provide greater transferability of learning for students than the study of isolated historical examples?

6. What is the value of a "generalization" to the learning process?

7. What are the dangers of generalizing related to

   – shallow thinking and low-level generalizations?
   – leaps of abstraction without supporting data?
   – bias in generalizing?

CHAPTER 4

Designing Interdisciplinary, Integrated Curricula

Teachers in elementary schools jump in and tenaciously pursue integrated unit teaching. The thought of reducing the burden of content by integrating subject matter is an appealing motivator. But the task has not been easy. A lack of well-articulated models has caused teachers to piece together integration techniques from trials and tidbits of training.

Heidi Hayes-Jacobs, a popular leader in the integrated curriculum movement, states that the integrated curriculum is not new. The last great innovative wave came in the late 1960s and early 1970s but was not successful because the structure of disciplines was lost and the abundance of activities in the unit contributed to a "potpourri" problem (Jacobs, 1994).

The disparate activities in these earlier forms of integration deflected learning from the content focus, and process participation became the end point for instruction. And in those days, there was little assessment for the quality of process performance. We struggle with the issue of quality performance assessment even today.

Student benefits from curriculum integration have become more apparent as teachers continue to explore the idea, and secondary teachers are now joining the quest. An interdisciplinary, integrated curriculum is a more difficult undertaking at the secondary level because of the traditional rigidity of subject area content expectations, some teacher attitudes toward change, class schedules, and issues related to collaboration and teaming.

This chapter will address the definition and value of integrated curriculum, review common forms of integration related to design sophistication, and present a step-by-step model for getting started. The chapter will end with answers to integration questions raised by elementary and secondary teachers.

Defining Interdisciplinary, Integrated Curricula

There are different forms of integration. A lower level form, which is more coordinated than the integrated form, relates facts and activities across subject areas to a common topic, such as "circus," "bears," "Africa," or "the Revolutionary period in American history." Students learn facts about the topic and develop their process skills through the varied activities, but an integrated focus to challenge higher level thinking is usually missing. Teachers often begin learning about curricular integration using this coordinated model and then progress to a higher form.

It is important for primary-grade teachers to be assured that teaching units on the circus, bears, or dinosaurs are fine, if teachers recognize that the major benefit will be the development of language skills around a motivational topic. And certainly, all students love the circus, bears, and dinosaurs! But teachers will also want to provide units that challenge the thinking abilities of their students. They could achieve both language development and higher level thinking in the same unit by linking a relevant concept to the topic study, such as "Hibernation" as a conceptual focus for the theme of "Bears in Winter." Or a unit designed specifically with a concept and theme could be undertaken at a different time to achieve the higher goal of conceptual integration.

The higher form of curriculum integration presented in this chapter rests on the following definition:

Curriculum integration is the organization of content under a common, abstract concept such as *interdependence* or *conflict*. The goal of integrated curricula is to illuminate more clearly the concept under study in relation to a significant theme, problem, or issue, through the application of higher level thought processes as students analyze, synthesize, and generalize from information to knowledge.

Interdisciplinary, as used in this chapter, refers to a variety of disciplines sharing a common, conceptual focus. The common focus on the concept—and theme, problem, or issue—contributes to deeper understanding and differentiates *interdisciplinary* from *multidisciplinary*. A well-designed integrated curriculum will also be interdisciplinary. The lower level coordinated curriculum is multidisciplinary because it lacks conceptual integration and focus.

In addition to the various levels of content integration, teachers make use of a form of process integration that is referred to as *integrated language arts*. Integrated language arts is the coordinated application of the language skills of reading, writing, listening, speaking, and thinking to a particular area of study, whether a piece of literature, an interdisciplinary content unit, or a motivational single topic unit focused on language development (see Figure 4.1). This chapter will deal with the design of the integrated content unit and discuss the application of language process skills.

The Integrated Curriculum Model

Chapter 3 presented the traditional model of topically based curriculum (Figure 3.1). The concept-based, integrated curriculum model presented in Figure 4.2 demonstrates that content from separate subject area disciplines can be integrated when focused on a common problem, theme, or issue linked to a major unifying concept. *It is the concept that draws thinking to higher cognitive levels.* This model also shows that process skills reside apart from the content because they develop internally in children and are nurtured and assessed quite differently than content. The process skills interact

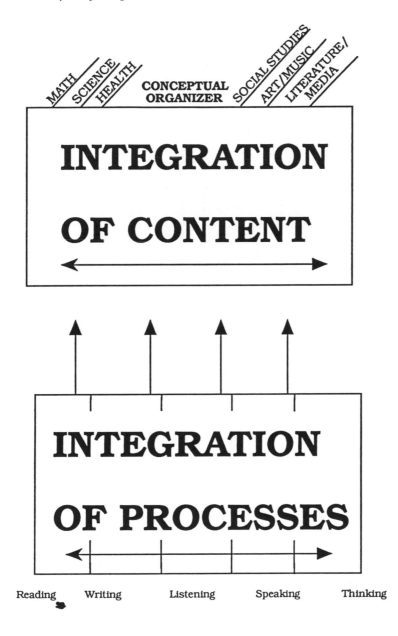

Figure 4.1. Process Integration and Content Integration

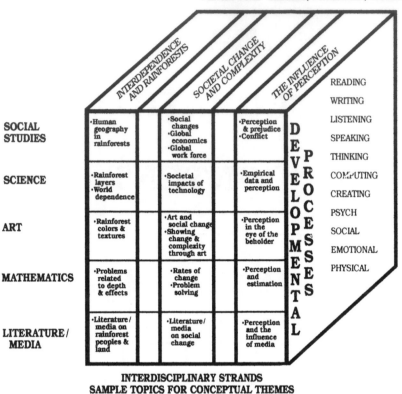

Figure 4.2. The Integrated Concept/Process Model

with content, however, and the mutual interdependence enhances conceptual and content understanding as well as process development.

Purpose and Value

Some educators feel that the purpose of integrated curricula is to obliterate the separate disciplines to avoid the current fragmentation of knowledge. I agree with Hayes-Jacobs, however, that the separate disciplines still have value and should not be sacrificed so readily.

One of the problems with a "seamless" curriculum is that, even though disciplines have many foundational concepts in common, they also have some discipline-specific concepts that would leave gaps in critical content knowledge if not addressed. Mathematics, for example, has the concepts of *number, order, ratio,* and *proportion,* which hold heavy content meaning. If subjects such as mathematics, literature, and art lose their content structure, they will perform poorly whether within, or outside of, integrated units.

The purpose of integrated curriculum goes back to the definition stated previously: "to illuminate more clearly the concept under study in relation to a significant theme, problem, or issue through the application of higher level thought processes."

Integration of curriculum should proceed at a pace that allows for developing understanding and consideration of the following questions:

- Which concepts and critical content *by subject area* do we consider to be essential as we enter the 21st century?
- What framework or criteria will we use to decide on the significant themes, problems, or issues around which curriculum is integrated?
- How will we ensure that we are including the agreed-upon concepts and critical content from the separate disciplines as we integrate our curriculum?
- If we move toward an issues orientation to the design of an integrated curriculum, what curriculum framework will ensure developing sophistication of conceptual understanding, critical content, and personal process skills?

As we continue to explore curriculum integration, the answers to the above issues will become clearer. There is no question that integrated curriculum offers great value for teaching and learning. Figure 4.3 lists often cited benefits.

Because the integrated curriculum format draws from a wider information base than the single subject area textbook, the teacher cannot hope to know all of the information prior to student engage-

STUDENT BENEFITS	EXPLANATION
• Reduces curricular fragmentation	– Facilitates curriculum connections
• Provides depth to teaching and learning	– Depth of thought and ideas, not depth of facts stacked higher
• Provides teaching and learning focus	– Teaching and learning are guided by the high-level generalizations arising from the concepts and critical content
• Engages students in active learning	– Students search for and construct knowledge using a variety of learning styles and modalities
• Challenges higher level thinking	– The abstract concept and generalizations force thinking to the analysis and synthesis levels
• Helps students connect knowledge	– The best minds rise above the facts and see patterns and relationships
• Addresses significant problems, issues, concepts	– Teacher-designed units typically address critical issues of life and our world
• Forces an answer to the relevancy question, "Why study these facts?"	– Facts are not ends but means to deeper understandings (The unit design provides teacher and learner focus.)
• Draws on multiple styles of learning	– Auditory, visual, and kinesthetic activities are designed to engage many different modalities

Figure 4.3. Benefits of Integrated Curriculum
SOURCE: Arizona Department of Education; used by permission.

ment. This allows for the freedom and flexibility to learn and ensures that students take responsibility for answering questions rather than depending on the teacher for the correct information.

In addition to the benefits for students, teachers find that the process of designing units facilitates their own development as learners. As they work collaboratively to plan the unit framework, teachers challenge their thinking in defining the critical outcomes for content and process development and in anticipating essential content learnings—the key generalizations. Integrated units provide pathways for creating new knowledge for teachers as well as for students.

Designing Integrated Teaching Units

Teachers who seek information on how to design an integrated curriculum ask for a step-by-step process that provides a model yet challenges their critical and creative thinking. Though I cringe to think that the model presented in this section will be looked upon as another Hunter-like set of steps, I also trust that teachers will see its value as a flexible springboard for engaging students in the design of integrated units as well as for engaging them in actual unit activities.

Table 4.1 lists 11 steps for designing integrated teaching units. I have been working with elementary- and secondary-grade teachers around the country for the past five years to develop and refine these steps. Next to each step are clarifying notes.

Other Notes on the Steps

Step   *Note*

(2) Step 2, identifying the concept, can precede steps 1 and 3 if you already have a conceptual focus.

(3) The more words you put into the topical theme, the tighter the time frame. For example, "The Westward Movement" as a theme could take six weeks or more, but "Pioneering Women of the Westward Movement" could be done in a much shorter time frame. Expansive theme titles that are not

Table 4.1. Steps for Designing Integrated Teaching Units

Steps	Notes
1. Select an *area of study*—a *topic of significance*	Examples: China, Africa, Seasons, Personal Health, Rainforests
2. Identify a *major concept* to focus the study.	Concepts were explained in Chapter 3. They are sometimes popularly referred to as "themes," but this book follows the definition in Chapter 3 so as not to confuse higher level concepts with lower level topics.
3. Using the area of study and the concept, develop a *topical theme* that frames the study and adheres to the time parameters.	Example: If "Rainforests" were the area of study, and "Interdependence" the focus concept, the topical theme could be "The Interdependence of Rainforests."
4. *Web the topics* for study, by subject or area, around the concept and theme.	This visual is the content web. Though "The Interdependence of Rainforests" lends itself to the study of topics by academic *subject*, "The Culture of Japan" as a theme might web more easily by *areas* of culture, such as language, customs, or foods.
5. Brainstorm some of the key *generalizations* that you would expect students to derive from the study.	Generalizations are essential transferable learnings, key understandings—the main ideas. Example: "Rainforest resources support diverse populations."
6. Brainstorm *guiding questions* to facilitate the study toward the unit outcome and generalizations.	This step is critical for ensuring that the study goes beyond lower level fact finding to the higher level understandings defined in the generalizations.

Table 4.1. (Continued)

Steps	Notes
7. Write the *unit outcome and activity (performance)* to stage the depth of learning and quality of performance.	The unit outcome and activity answer the question, "What do I want students to *know* and *do* as a result of this integrated study?"
8. Design the rubric (criteria or traits, a scale of measure, and a standard) to assess the unit outcome and performance activity.	The rubric is the assessment instrument. Rubrics continue to improve as educators work to identify the indicators of quality work and performance. Rubrics are discussed in greater detail in Chapter 5.
9. Write *directed outcomes* that students must know or be able to do as they progress through the unit.	Directed outcomes are what the students must know or be able to do as a result of "direct instruction" from the teacher. For example, if the unit outcome calls for "analysis" of content material, the students must be taught how to analyze to a set of criteria and a critical thinking standard.
10. Decide on a higher level *thinking skill* that can be taught and infused into the unit work.	As the unit is focused toward generalizations, the higher level thinking is a natural part of the unit and may, or may not, need direct instruction. Dialogue, discussion questions, and self-reflection develop thinking.
11. Work between the concept, theme, and outcomes to decide on day-by-day *activities* to carry out the learning.	This is the daily lesson plan. If the unit is three weeks, then there would be 15 days of lessons. It is in the lesson activities that the students' *personal process and performance skills* are developed.

correlated to the teaching time frame are a typical error of beginning designers.

(3) Though it is not always necessary to repeat the concept as part of the topical theme, doing so helps to mentally "bridge" the topic to the conceptual focus.

(5) Generalizations—essential content summaries—are the component that we seem to have lost in the traditional curriculum. It is critical that teachers think through the instruction and answer the relevancy questions—"So what?" and "Why study these facts?"—for guiding content teaching. Generalizations are often the most difficult step in integrated unit design for beginners.

(6) Once the teacher knows the purpose and procedure for writing guiding questions, the students can assist with this step.

(8) Chapter 5 provides examples of assessment rubrics for evaluating performance on the unit outcome and activity.

(9) Another example of directed outcome would be "producing the form for haiku," if haiku writing were included in the unit.

(11) The daily lesson activities send the students on the search for knowledge. They draw on many different learning styles and modalities to construct and display knowledge.

There are popular educational philosophies today that assert that students should go on the search for knowledge based on their own interests and that the teacher should not set the topic of study. This view also asserts that the search process is the issue of importance and that the content is only a vehicle for facilitating the development of the internal process skills. As with most trends, I take a balanced position and believe that opportunities for both open-ended and structured search processes are important to the educational program.

The 11 steps presented in this book provide structure to the content learning for several reasons:

- A planned curriculum that develops both process and content sophistication will achieve greater results than a happenstance content curriculum that is focused mainly on a student's process development. Both content and process development are important.

- When teachers have not thought through the content lessons, they often miss the higher level essential learnings for students. The activities often dominate learning—and depth of content understanding is lost.

- Most schools and districts require a core content curriculum. Even if teachers wished to continually present curriculum in open-ended contexts, mandated requirements for content force a structure.

Sample Unit Overview Webs

When teachers begin learning how to write integrated curricula, they often start with a lower cognitive form that coordinates fact-based study and activities to a topic, such as the circus, bears, or Africa. An example of this multidisciplinary, coordinated curriculum is shown in Figure 4.4. Primary-grade students, especially, can benefit from these topic units because a primary emphasis is on developing language. The trouble with this design is that if it is used exclusively, it does not help students understand the topic in relation to a higher order concept. Thinking remains at the level of isolated facts and activities. Synthesis of information to the abstract level of essential learnings is lost.

It is a simple matter to rework a topic unit into a higher order unit by deciding on a concept to link with the topic. The activities of the unit are then focused toward understanding the relationship of the chosen concept and the topical theme. For example, an integrating concept for the theme of "The Circus" might be "Performance," or for a theme on "African Art," the concept of "Representations" would be appropriate.

At this point, it might be helpful to review some definitions that are critical to understanding this section:

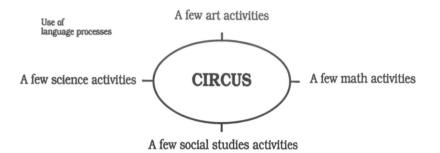

Figure 4.4. Multidisciplinary, Coordinated Activities Curriculum

- Universal *Concept*—A mental construct that is timeless and abstract: The examples of the concept may vary in content, but the base descriptors are the same. Examples: symmetry, cycle, conflict, interdependence.
- *Generalization*—Two or more concepts stated in a relationship. Example: Freedom is the basis for democracy.
- Topical *Theme*—The title of a unit of study. It may, or may not, state the concept that is a focus for the unit study as a part of the title. Examples: "Symmetry and Balance in Motion"; "Our Town."
- *Topics*—The content to be experienced through the unit activities. The topics are brainstormed on the overview web under each subject or area surrounding the theme.

Figure 4.5 shows a higher level, integrated unit design. This unit uses a topical theme ("Our Town"), but the content and activities of the unit view this theme in relationship to the concept of "Change" over time. This design forces thinking to the abstract level as students arrive inductively at generalizations and principles drawn from the concept of change as related to the content examples experienced throughout the unit.

The design in Figure 4.5 meets the criteria of a strong interdisciplinary, integrated unit. Using the definition of integrated curriculum that was presented earlier in this chapter, the unit "Our Town" is a vehicle for students to learn higher level understandings related

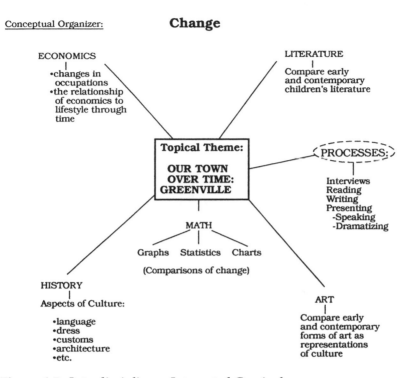

Figure 4.5. Interdisciplinary, Integrated Curriculum

to the concept of "Change" over time. This unit also meets the additional criteria of a strong, integrated unit because each of the subject areas has depth of study—it does not comprise a few activities. The conceptual focus of "Change" brings cohesion to the unit. The students know the focus for learning, but the search for knowledge is their responsibility.

Figures 4.6 to 4.11 are samples of the brainstormed concept/content webs that elementary and secondary teachers have developed in planning integrated units. Each figure has been chosen to illustrate one or more of the steps for design. Accompanying each figure is a discussion of the illustrative points.

The webs show the initial brainstorming efforts in planning the *content focus* for the unit study. It is important to realize that these figures do not intend to convey the personal process skills that

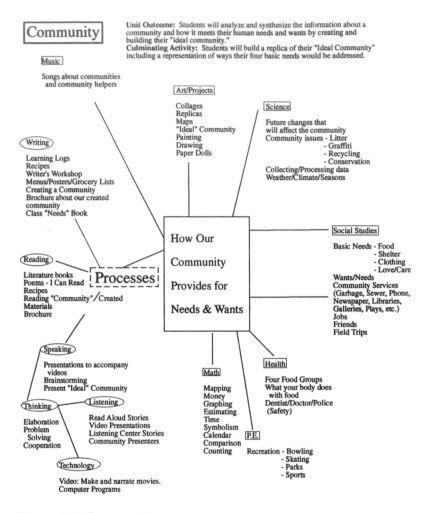

Figure 4.6. Community
SOURCE: Kathryn Southerland, Amy Evans Smith, and Hilah Cochrane
(Crownhill Elementary School, Bremerton, Washington); used by permission.

students will develop and apply to the content study. Those will
appear in the daily lessons through a variety of process activities such
as drama, debates, panel presentations, technology displays, plays,
or musical, oral, or written presentations.

A common area of study in the primary grades relates to the community. In Figure 4.6, students analyze how communities meet the needs and wants of its citizens. The study is culminated when students construct a replica of their "Ideal Community," which represents four basic needs being addressed. In this overview map, the teachers identify the language arts processes students will apply throughout the unit. You will notice some of the subject areas also contain process skills. They can be identified by their *-ing* endings, such as painting in art and graphing in mathematics. These subjects are process as well as content based, and it is common for teachers to bring both into the unit overview in these cases.

Figure 4.7 states the theme in the form of a question. This is a provocative way to state an issue of significance and engage students' interest in the study. The unit outcome and activity for this unit states, "Analyze whether freedom still exists in America, in order to evaluate your rights as an American citizen, by researching a recent court case regarding the Bill of Rights and debating the decision."

The guiding questions that were developed to focus the study of this unit toward essential learnings, or generalizations, are open ended and allow the students to go on a search for knowledge. The questions challenge the students' desire to know:

- How is freedom defined?
- How can you measure freedom?
- Is freedom a human concept?
- How is censorship controlled?
- How does the Supreme Court regulate freedom?
- Are we born free?
- Does freedom still exist?
- How have the opinions of freedom changed?
- Have we gained or lost freedom? Explain.
- How is freedom regulated by society?

In Figure 4.8, an English teacher and a music teacher teamed up to write a unit related to the Civil War. The music teacher wanted to have students explore blues as an expression of conflict following the

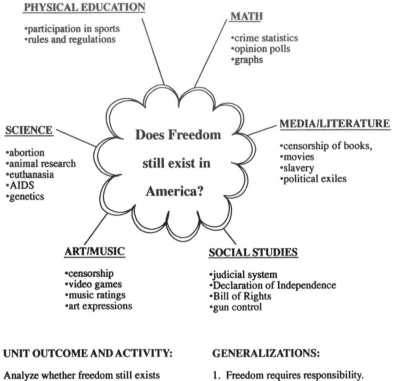

PHYSICAL EDUCATION
•participation in sports
•rules and regulations

MATH
•crime statistics
•opinion polls
•graphs

SCIENCE
•abortion
•animal research
•euthanasia
•AIDS
•genetics

Does Freedom

still exist in

America?

MEDIA/LITERATURE
•censorship of books,
•movies
•slavery
•political exiles

ART/MUSIC
•censorship
•video games
•music ratings
•art expressions

SOCIAL STUDIES
•judicial system
•Declaration of Independence
•Bill of Rights
•gun control

UNIT OUTCOME AND ACTIVITY:

Analyze whether freedom still exists
in America, in order to evaluate your
rights as an American citizen, by
researching a recent court case
regarding the Bill of Rights and
debating the decision.

GENERALIZATIONS:

1. Freedom requires responsibility.
2. Freedom involves choices.
3. Freedom can be taken away.
4. Freedom is a matter of interpretation.
5. Order requires rules.

Figure 4.7. Does Freedom Exist?
SOURCE: Kathryn B. Folley, Emily F. Hamby, Kelli M. Such, and Lisa A.
Rotunda (Drayton Hall Middle School, Charleston, South Carolina); used
by permission.

Civil War. The English teacher wanted students to understand the
issues of the conflict and relate to a soldier's point of view concerning
conflict resolution. The unit outcome and activity that end the study

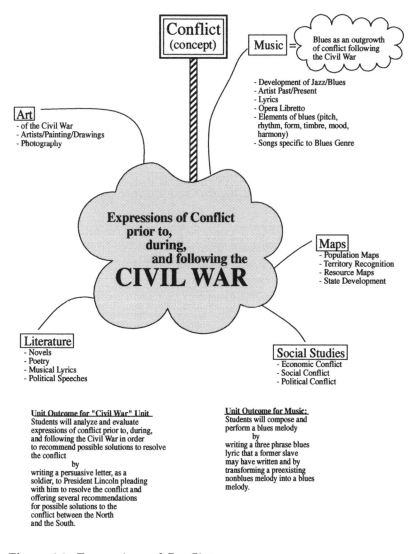

Figure 4.8. Expressions of Conflict
SOURCE: Mary Rein and Deborah Vaughn (Clear Creek Elementary, Silverdale, Washington); used by permission.

are high-level performances that require both content and process sophistication.

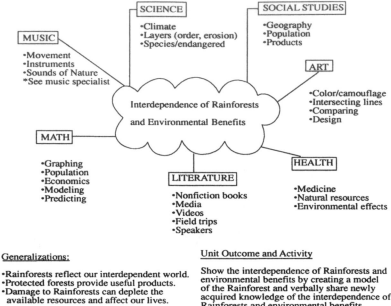

Figure 4.9. Interdependence of Rain Forests
SOURCE: Shari Hastings, Toni Cummings, and Kristin Martinson (Sherwood Forest Elementary, Federal Way Public Schools, Federal Way, Washington); used by permission.

The unit shown in Figure 4.9 is a popular unit in schools today. A danger is that it is being used at too many grade levels. I have seen this unit at grades 2, 4, 6, and 7 in the same school district. It is a valuable unit of study, however, and with communication between teachers alleviating overkill, this unit has great potential for motivating students. Notice how the generalizations guide learning. Students will discover other generalizations as they search for knowledge. The generalizations are the synthesis of learning. They relate two or more concepts into a higher level statement with universal and timeless application, as noted (Figure 4.9).

In Figure 4.10, note the high-level generalizations. Often when teachers first begin writing generalizations, they are drawn from a surface level of thought. As they become more accustomed to synthesizing the learnings from content, the generalizations become more sophisticated. As students progress through the grades, the generalizations they derive should parallel the increasing depth of the content under study.

Figure 4.11 shows that teachers are drawn to issues of social significance when asked to design units of study. These issues need to be addressed in classrooms. Violence in America is certainly a theme of great concern to students, parents, and teachers today. This is one of the best uses of integrated curriculum. Students view complex issues from multiple perspectives and develop problem-solving skills, which are essential to effective citizenship.

Figure 4.12 shows how classroom content can be incorporated into integrated, interdisciplinary units. The concept is "Paradigm Shifts," and the subconcepts of "Innovation," "Power," and "Perception" are addressed through the means of various subjects and topics. An important point in this example is the manner in which teachers asked students to transfer learning from the Renaissance period to a contemporary example. This provides students with the understanding that paradigm shifts are timeless, and allows them to generalize to the essential learnings.

Cultural themes, such as the one shown in Figure 4.13 on exploring the impact of French culture on North American culture, teaches students how interacting cultures influence each other. Cultures are compared and studied through various cultural aspects, from language, to trade, to technology.

A final overview web, shown in Figure 4.14, takes a mathematics focus with the theme "Measurement in Our World." It shows the integration of mathematics throughout our lives as we make sense of

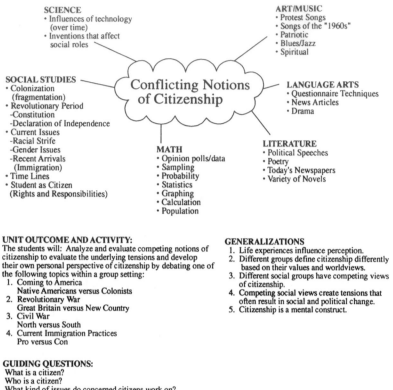

SCIENCE
- Influences of technology (over time)
- Inventions that affect social roles

ART/MUSIC
- Protest Songs
- Songs of the "1960s"
- Patriotic
- Blues/Jazz
- Spiritual

SOCIAL STUDIES
- Colonization (fragmentation)
- Revolutionary Period
  -Constitution
  -Declaration of Independence
- Current Issues
  -Racial Strife
  -Gender Issues
  -Recent Arrivals (Immigration)
- Time Lines
- Student as Citizen (Rights and Responsibilities)

Conflicting Notions of Citizenship

LANGUAGE ARTS
- Questionnaire Techniques
- News Articles
- Drama

MATH
- Opinion polls/data
- Sampling
- Probability
- Statistics
- Graphing
- Calculation
- Population

LITERATURE
- Political Speeches
- Poetry
- Today's Newspapers
- Variety of Novels

UNIT OUTCOME AND ACTIVITY:
The students will: Analyze and evaluate competing notions of citizenship to evaluate the underlying tensions and develop their own personal perspective of citizenship by debating one of the following topics within a group setting:
1. Coming to America
   Native Americans versus Colonists
2. Revolutionary War
   Great Britain versus New Country
3. Civil War
   North versus South
4. Current Immigration Practices
   Pro versus Con

GENERALIZATIONS
1. Life experiences influence perception.
2. Different groups define citizenship differently based on their values and worldviews.
3. Different social groups have competing views of citizenship.
4. Competing social views create tensions that often result in social and political change.
5. Citizenship is a mental construct.

GUIDING QUESTIONS:
What is a citizen?
Who is a citizen?
What kind of issues do concerned citizens work on?
What do you think a good citizen does? Justify your view.
How does society reward or judge good/bad citizens?
Name some good citizens and state why they are "good."
In what ways do citizens work on their own and/or in a group.
Why was there a fragmentation of the colonies?
What does "Justice for All" mean?
How is citizenship defined in other cultures?
Are there some cultures where citizenship might be more readily agreed upon?
In what kind of countries might citizenship be more difficult to define?

Figure 4.10. Conflicting Notions of Citizenship
SOURCE: Kay Gifford, Karen Nelson, and Dawn Schaenzer (Cedar Mill Elementary, Beaverton, Oregon); John Seggie (Vose Elementary, Beaverton, Oregon); and Judy VanScoter (West Tualitin View, Beaverton, Oregon); used by permission.

the world. The concept is "Relationships," an appropriate lens for using the process tools of mathematics to create mental connections. You will notice that content webs such as those presented in this book

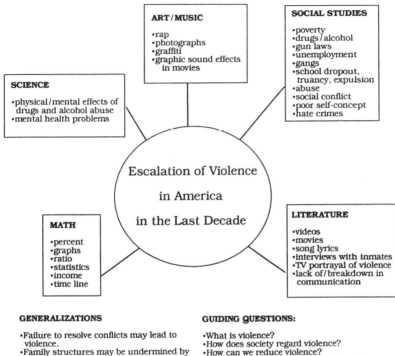

ART/MUSIC

•rap
•photographs
•graffiti
•graphic sound effects
  in movies

SOCIAL STUDIES

•poverty
•drugs/alcohol
•gun laws
•unemployment
•gangs
•school dropout,
  truancy, expulsion
•abuse
•social conflict
•poor self-concept
•hate crimes

SCIENCE

•physical/mental effects of
  drugs and alcohol abuse
•mental health problems

Escalation of Violence

in America

in the Last Decade

MATH

•percent
•graphs
•ratio
•statistics
•income
•time line

LITERATURE

•videos
•movies
•song lyrics
•interviews with inmates
•TV portrayal of violence
•lack of/breakdown in
  communication

GENERALIZATIONS

•Failure to resolve conflicts may lead to
  violence.
•Family structures may be undermined by
  violence.
•Drug/alcohol abuse can lead to violence.

GUIDING QUESTIONS:

•What is violence?
•How does society regard violence?
•How can we reduce violence?
•Is violence restricted to certain groups?
•Does the media's portrayal of violence affect
  society?
•Is violence a form of control?
•Is violence entertaining?

Figure 4.11. Violence in America
SOURCE: Angela Mills, Betty Hazel, Ellamae Washington, Evelyn
Workman, and Sally Newell (Toole Middle School, Charleston, South
Carolina); used by permission.

show the *applications* of mathematics. Some mathematics teachers
feel they are not helping students learn mathematics unless the
students are doing algorithms as the end product. The value of using
mathematics to extend understanding of topics and issues throughout an interdisciplinary unit is that it takes the algorithms off the page
and brings them to life through relevant application. Algorithms are
a tool, not an end product.

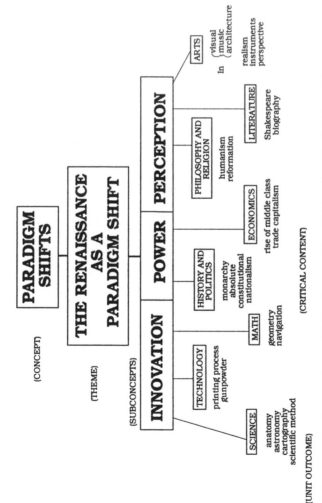

(CONCEPT)

PARADIGM SHIFTS

(THEME)

THE RENAISSANCE AS A PARADIGM SHIFT

(SUBCONCEPTS)

INNOVATION   **POWER**   **PERCEPTION**

TECHNOLOGY
printing process
gunpowder

SCIENCE
anatomy
astronomy
cartography
scientific method

MATH
geometry
navigation

HISTORY AND POLITICS
monarchy
absolute
constitutional
nationalism

ECONOMICS
rise of middle class
trade capitalism

PHILOSOPHY AND RELIGION
humanism
reformation

LITERATURE
Shakespeare
biography

ARTS
visual
music
architecture
In
realism
instruments
perspective

(CRITICAL CONTENT)

(UNIT OUTCOME)

Students will analyze the major changes of the Renaissance and their effects in order to identify their parallels in current society by researching and role playing a key Renaissance contributor, explaining his/her contribution, and comparing it with a modern/current change.

Figure 4.12. Paradigm Shifts

SOURCE: Nancy Hooper and Pat Bennett-Forman (North Kitsap School District, Poulsbo, Washington) and Gayl Cundiff (Chimacum School District, Chimacum, Washington); used by permission.

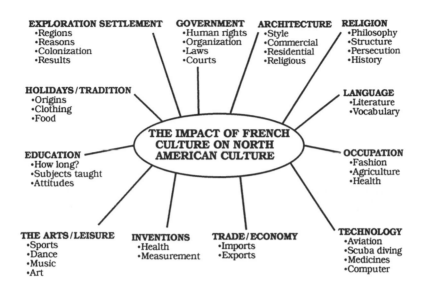

EXPLORATION SETTLEMENT
•Regions
•Reasons
•Colonization
•Results

GOVERNMENT
•Human rights
•Organization
•Laws
•Courts

ARCHITECTURE
•Style
•Commercial
•Residential
•Religious

RELIGION
•Philosophy
•Structure
•Persecution
•History

HOLIDAYS / TRADITION
•Origins
•Clothing
•Food

LANGUAGE
•Literature
•Vocabulary

THE IMPACT OF FRENCH CULTURE ON NORTH AMERICAN CULTURE

EDUCATION
•How long?
•Subjects taught
•Attitudes

OCCUPATION
•Fashion
•Agriculture
•Health

THE ARTS / LEISURE
•Sports
•Dance
•Music
•Art

INVENTIONS
•Health
•Measurement

TRADE / ECONOMY
•Imports
•Exports

TECHNOLOGY
•Aviation
•Scuba diving
•Medicines
•Computer

UNIT OUTCOME / ACTIVITY

Students will evaluate the impact of French culture on North American culture by researching, presenting and defending as an "expert" their acquired knowledge (chosen topic) at a French-American Summit.

GENERALIZATIONS

1. Cultures affect one another.
2. Merging cultures influence change.
3. Culture has social, political, and economic ramifications.
4. Merging cultures create paradigm shifts.
5. Cultural differences develop out of need.
6. Cultures affect our interdependent world.

GUIDING QUESTIONS

1. How do cultures affect one another?
2. How do merging cultures influence change?
3. What are some social, political, and economic ramifications of culture?
4. Why do merging cultures create paradigm shifts?
5. How would need affect culture?
6. In what ways do cultures affect our interdependent world?

Figure 4.13. The Impact of French Culture
SOURCE: Sue Pasqualicchio (Dubose Middle School, Summerville, South Carolina) and Laura Childers and Camilla D. Groome (Alston Middle School, Summerville, South Carolina); used by permission.

Pitfalls in Unit Design

Effective curriculum design requires general knowledge of content, higher level thinking and writing abilities, and multiple strate-

Figure 4.14. Measurement in Our World
SOURCE: John Miller (Illahee Junior High, Federal Way, Washington), adapted from the mapping of Jim Roberts, Jeanne Gordon, Jan Asher, and Wande Siebert (Hauser Junior and Senior High Schools, Hope, Indiana); used by permission.

gies for engaging students in study and performance. Teachers must think through the content to the higher level generalizations, or essential learnings. They must have enough skill in writing to be able to express the structure, outcomes, and assessment standards for units of work.

Failure to ask the following questions in the design of integrated units leads to common pitfalls:

- Which concept will most effectively capture the direction and significance of the unit when paired with the theme and subject area topics?

  - For example, if the unit theme was "Homelessness in America," then a concept such as "Poverty" or "Humanitarianism" would be appropriate. The concept of "Hunger" would be too narrow, and the concept of "Interdependence" would not provide a clear link to the theme.

- Why study these facts? What are some of the generalizations and principles that students might derive?
- Is the unit cohesive and focused around the concept and theme?
- Is the theme too broad for the study's time frame?
- Is the unit motivating and meaningful for students?
- Do the different subjects or areas of study work together to provide depth of understanding?
- Are the unit outcome, and directed outcomes, clear and significant?
- Is the performance assessment directly tied to the unit outcome and activity? Do you measure what you wish to measure? Are the criteria and standards set for both the content and the process outcomes what the students know and can do?
- Do the activities use a broad range of process skills?
- Do the activities lead students to an understanding of the summary generalizations, or have the activities become the ends of learning?
- Have the activities remained true to the concept and theme?
- Is the study in each discipline of sufficient depth that it could stand alone as a valid study?

- Is there a balance in the unit between increasing sophistication in conceptual and content understanding related to a significant theme of study and increasing sophistication in process and presentation skills such as language use, thinking ability, and personal performance?

Questions and Responses: Elementary Schools

1. Why should interdisciplinary units have both a concept and a theme?

Response: A concept by itself does not provide enough focus to the study across disciplines. A topical theme carries the idea of the concept into a form that is understandable and approachable for students and sets the parameters for the content study.

Example:

> **Concept:**   Culture
> **Theme:**   "African and Japanese Art as Expressions of
> Culture"

The theme brings focus and direction to the study of "Culture." The theme can also be stated as a question to engage the students in searching for knowledge: "In what ways are African and Japanese art expressive of culture?"

2. How does the concept/thematic unit design compare with the project approach and inquiry unit designs?

Response: Both the project approach and inquiry design models are open-ended frameworks that allow the student to go on the search for knowledge and construct personal meaning. The emphasis is on investigation and collaborative inquiry around a major topic of interest to the students. Sometimes the inquiry may be around a concept alone such as "Change." Harste and Burke (1993) stress the importance of teacher planning in helping students define the inquiry questions related to the topic under study. They suggest using the disciplines as a viewing lens: "What generalizations, principles, or conclusions would a scientist want us to learn? . . . a psychologist? . . . an artist?" (p. 3).

Because the project approach and inquiry models value the process of open-ended knowledge construction emanating from the interests of children, they do not address the issue of K-12 curriculum articulation.

The concept/thematic unit design presented in this chapter also sends students on a search for knowledge and a personal construction of meaning, but the search is focused on inquiry leading to higher level essential learnings related to the concept and theme, as opposed to open-ended inquiry. This focus allows for an articulation of concepts and themes through the grades and protects a balance of process and content. The integrity of student responsibility for learning and knowledge construction is still protected, however.

3. Can I use open-ended, as well as structured, unit designs in my classroom?

Response: Certainly. Both forms have unique benefits in the learning environment. The task will be twofold:

- To lay out the units of instruction so that the district or school framework for content and process development is achieved
- To provide opportunities for open-ended, experiential learning

4. How can I engage students in the planning of the units?

Response: Once you are comfortable with the components of unit design, you can ask students to plan the unit overview with you. Find out what students know, from their background knowledge, about the concept and theme. They can help define topics to be studied related to the concept and theme, and can assist in developing the guiding questions. Remember, though, that you need to make certain there are open-ended guiding questions that will cause students to arrive at essential learnings—those transferable lessons of life that help students make conceptual and real sense of their world.

5. How long should units last?

Response: The time varies. A kindergarten or first-grade unit may last only a few days to a week; a secondary unit developed by an interdisciplinary team may last 12 weeks.

6. How should I begin moving toward integrated instruction?

Response: Begin with a single unit. Learn from the 11 steps for designing integrated units and then develop a second unit.

7. How many units might I introduce in a year?

Response: This would depend on the length of your units, but monthly unit activity is common. Units usually last from three to six weeks in intermediate grades and beyond. Primary-grade units may be shorter in duration.

8. How can I structure my day for direct and integrated instruction?

Response: Teacher preference plays heavily into this question, but I prefer direct instruction or **cooperative learning** activities and flexible skill groups in the morning, and integrated unit work in the afternoon.

Direct instruction means teacher direction of skills to develop reading, writing, and speaking—or teacher presentation of content information critical to the unit work—that students would not be seeking themselves. It is important to select carefully the content information presented in direct instruction as opposed to content searched out by the student. The direct instruction of content is often for a motivational purpose or establishes the skill foundation for the student search.

Integrated unit work in the afternoon often incorporates the skills and content information presented in the morning. Reading, writing, and speaking and mathematics skills are applied in the context of the integrated units.

9. I have difficulty finding a theme that lends itself well to the study of integrated science and social studies.

Response: Because social studies is oriented toward culture and humanity, it is sometimes difficult to bridge to the physical and nonhuman branches of science. You will find that environmental themes, such as "Pollution as a Threat to Humanity," lend themselves well to social studies as well as science because they have strong ramifications for both domains. We should not "stretch" to try and make a subject fit into a theme. This dilutes the integrity of the study as a whole. As Jacobs (1989) states, "Validity within the disciplines requires . . . that concepts identified are not merely related to their subjects but are important to them" (p. 27). You will find that units with a science theme incorporate mathematics, health, vocations, and technology quite easily. Units with a social studies theme readily incorporate the arts, music, literature, and media. The thematic focus of units can be alternated throughout a year. Mathematics and language process skills apply across all curricular areas, however.

10. How can I manage all of the content and process instruction mandated by our district and state frameworks and still teach by integrated units?

Response: Through personal empowerment, understanding, and organization.

Personal empowerment: You are the lead designer of curriculum and instruction for the 21st century in your classroom. Districts and states provide frameworks of content, process, and student outcomes to assist you but recognize that these documents are only guides. Because you have a professional responsibility to work toward the broad content and process outcomes outlined in these frameworks, you need certain understandings.

Understanding: State and district curriculum frameworks today focus on *Student Outcomes,* or *Goals,* which state the desired process
skills, such as "Communicate at high levels." In addition, there are
usually one or two outcomes, that call for student understanding of
major subject area concepts and principles.

Aligned to the student outcomes, subject area frameworks identify
major concepts as well as process (performance) expectations. The
district framework usually identifies some of the critical content by
grade, or grade-level groupings, such as kindergarten to grade 2.

Organization: Frameworks do not usually differentiate clearly between concepts, critical content, and developmental processes. To
plan the curricular program for the year, teachers need to identify
the concepts, critical content, and developmental processes outlined
in the framework.

Less is more: You can reduce the critical content by framing the
content examples under organizing concepts.

Organization:

1. List the concepts that are identified in the district frameworks
   for each academic subject; if given, note the critical content by
   topic under each concept.
2. Look for concepts that cut across disciplines and develop *topically based themes* to frame the conceptual units of study.
3. When developing the units for the year, incorporate the process
   skills, and design lessons, so that the desired student performances are achieved and displayed.
4. Map out a sequence of integrated concept/thematic units for
   the year. For critical content that cannot be addressed within the
   context of a unit, plan for a single topic focus.

**11. Is it always necessary to design integrated units that relate to
the content of the district curriculum frameworks?**

Response: Teachers need the latitude to design units of interest
and relevance to students that may not fall within the mandated
frameworks. Some of the unit overview webs provided in this book
are examples of teachers choosing to design a unit that deviated, such

as "Escalation of Violence in America," "Conflicting Notions of Citizenship," and so on. Teachers balance the professional responsibility to address the content mandated in curricular frameworks with the need to explore issues critical and meaningful for society.

Questions and Responses: Secondary Schools

1. Some of our teachers do not see any need to change from the traditional approaches to curriculum and instruction. How can we bring them on board?

Response: The first step in encouraging change is education. Discussion of articles that address current and critical issues in education from leading journals such as *Phi Delta Kappan* and *Educational Leadership* stimulates thinking.

Teachers should also subscribe to their field-specific journal, such as *Social Education*, the excellent publication from the National Council of Social Studies. Books and articles that share current information on economic, social, and political trends provide additional insight into change. Curriculum is largely shaped by these trends and teachers need to be aware of the issues so that special interest groups do not take advantage of an awareness vacuum to install narrow interpretations into curricular materials.

Chapter 1 addressed the issues of staff change. It can take three or four years to change a person's mental paradigm. Teachers are more receptive to change when they see that content still has a place in the classroom. The growing emphasis on process outcomes in teaching has caused some teachers to be concerned that content will be lost. They need to see the balance between process and content. Time spent in staff meetings discussing educational trends and the need for change is an invaluable first step.

2. How do we organize as a staff for interdisciplinary teaching?

Response: There are many different models, from a multidisciplinary format with two teachers in different fields coordinating topics they are teaching—such as a literature and history teacher dealing with the Renaissance period at the same time in the year—to higher level integrated models that use interdisciplinary teaching teams organized under theme-based, and concept-based, curriculum strands.

There are many examples of schools around the United States that have altered their class schedules to facilitate interdisciplinary teaching. Two examples are **block scheduling** of two or three subjects and the "school-within-a-school" concept that sets up interdisciplinary teams of teachers with a set number of students who design the minischool schedule according to the curricular and instructional plan. The degree to which a school decides to transform its curricular and instructional program is determined by the school and parent community. District-level support is crucial.

3. What issues should we consider in determining our readiness to transform our curricular and instructional program?

Response:

- How committed is the staff to making change? Do you need to start with education and discussion as first steps?
- What leadership resources do you have? How knowledgeable are leaders in the following:

  - current trends
  - curriculum design for the 21st century
  - articulating the horizontal and vertical curricular content program
  - integrating curriculum
  - process teaching to outcomes
  - teaching to higher order thinking
  - scheduling
  - teaming

- consensus building
- conflict resolution

The issues listed above will unfold as teachers learn by doing, but leaders need to have baseline knowledge, or know where to find the resource help, so that valuable time is not wasted in committee.

- Do you know where to find the human and material resources you will need to plan a high-quality curricular and instructional program?

4. I am a mathematics teacher. I don't have time for participating in an integrated curriculum because I have to prepare my students for the next level of mathematics, and it takes a full year.

Response: The *Professional Standards for Teaching Mathematics* (1991), published by the National Council of Teachers of Mathematics, stresses the importance of mathematical reasoning and problem solving as well as communicating and using mathematics in real-world applications. Because integrated units revolve around life problems, issues, and concepts, they provide a fertile context for the relevant application of mathematics.

Teachers are realizing that their job is not just to prepare students for the next level of mathematics but to prepare them for a life that makes use of mathematics. Because of the heavy emphasis in traditional instruction on the isolated drill and practice with algorithms, students often fail to see the relevance of their learning. Perhaps if students become personally engaged with the applications of the algorithm, they will need less drill and practice to gain understanding.

Mathematics teachers in the changing paradigm realize that their job is not just to prepare students to perfunctorily follow formulas and solve equations. Their job is to provide students with the process tools of mathematics and to see that those tools are used to solve real-world problems. Progressive teachers of mathematics extend understanding of topics across subject areas. They help students reason mathematically. Mathematics is a process tool just as language is a process tool. And, like language, mathematics is a form of both thought and communication.

5. How should our interdisciplinary team decide on a concept and theme for our unit?

Response: As stated earlier, it is important for separate disciplines to identify their organizing concepts and critical content by topics prior to designing the integrated curriculum. Social studies, as representative of culture and people, and science, as representative of the natural and physical world, often provide the base for identifying an organizing concept and theme. The humanities—art, philosophy, music, literature, drama, dance, and so on—usually fit well into cultural themes. Technology, mathematics, and health work well in the physical and natural world themes. Mathematics and language process skills are applied across subject areas to extend understanding.

English teachers expect the language skills to be applied across subjects. Mathematics teachers have not always viewed their subject as a process skill to be applied to topics in other classrooms and subjects. This may be one reason they sometimes feel discomfort when participating in the design of an integrated, interdisciplinary unit.

6. How do we decide what is critical content within our subject area?

Response: Answer the following questions related to the topics in your subject area:

- What are your course outcomes? What do you want students to know and be able to do by the time they leave your course?
- What content is mandated by district or state curriculum frameworks?
- What do students need to know to progress to the next level of understanding in your discipline?
- What do you, as a professional, feel students need to know to understand your discipline?

- Can you articulate for your students *why* you have selected the different topics of critical content? How will your selection benefit students?

7. Will my subject area (physical education, health, anatomy/ physiology, mathematics, and so on) get to be the main focus of a concept/thematic unit? Do I always have to work under a social studies or science theme?

Response: There are times when a strong unit can be designed around a physical education or health concept. An example would be a unit based on the concept of "Fitness." As a content field, health has many concepts that would serve to organize a relevant interdisciplinary study: disease, organism, cycle, fitness, and so on. Because social studies and science are broader fields, however, they contain a greater range of concepts and themes. It is easier for the elective subjects to fit into the broader frames than the converse.

Physical education, health, and family life teachers can team to design powerfully relevant units for students based on personal, family, and community issues. It is effective to have flexible team formations. It doesn't work to force physical education into a science-based unit, for example, if the theme and concept are not appropriate. It is better to form the interdisciplinary team based on members who can contribute increased perspective to the question under study.

8. I teach world languages. How does that fit in?

Response: World languages are based in culture and will fit into any social studies unit that organizes around a culture-based concept. They will also fit into science themes. The language, people, and land of the culture under study will provide the setting.

9. How about technology? How does that fit in?

Response: Technology is a tool to access, ponder, and portray information. Like mathematics, it is applied across the fields of study to extend understanding and display learning. The uses of technology in society often fit into both social studies- and science-based units. And certainly, with the increasing importance of technology in science and society, it is a key player in many units.

10. If I take time for integrated units, I won't be able to cover the material in my textbook.

Response: If you compare the thickness and size of a textbook today with a textbook from 1980, you will likely see a significant increase in size. One publisher is now sending out two volumes of world history for one course. If you look at the depth of treatment related to critical issues in history, you will find abbreviated summaries of key events compared with a 1980 text. If you feel compelled to "cover the book," you are essentially skimming over surface data, losing many students along the way, and sacrificing the development of each child's personal process skills.

Belief in the new paradigm "less is more" challenges you to focus curriculum and instruction around significant concepts and themes. Your textbook will be one of many resources that students will use as they search for knowledge. The classroom is characterized by small-group and individual activity, and process activities such as drama, debates, dialogues, artistic renderings, and music. Students will have greater retention of the key concepts and critical issues because of their personal involvement in learning. By participating in integrated, interdisciplinary units, students will have the benefit of multiple perspectives and greater depth of understanding.

Transitional Integrated Curricula

We cannot leave this chapter on integrated curricula without looking at some of the secondary school models that would be considered transitional (as opposed to traditional or transformational) under Bill Spady's definition (1991)—transitional in the sense that they emphasize future life role, process skills. One example of this form is the Career Path model.

It is important to study the transitional models because they provide a more relevant context for learning and problem solving than the traditional subject-divided curricula. Just as concepts and interesting unit themes provide a rich context for focused, higher level learning in the classrooms, an organizing theme provides focus and relevance for an articulated and coordinated educational program. Transitional models, such as the Career Path, provide a meaningful, future-oriented framework for learning. Content is applied in a purposeful context and the relevancy question, "So what?" has an answer.

As you read about the designs that follow, think of the questions that need to be addressed by teachers, administrators, and parents as they articulate critical concepts, content, and processes under the organizing theme. Work still needs to be done in the area of articulating critical concepts and content to design relevant and meaningful integrated units within the career strands.

David Douglas High School, Portland, Oregon

David Douglas High School has developed a Career Path model of curriculum called "Project Stars" (1992) that allows students to select into a four-year academic/career plan framed by one of the following career fields:

- Production and technology
- Social and human services
- Environmental, physical, and health sciences
- Hospitality and recreation
- Marketing and business
- Arts and communication

Within each of these fields, there are three "orbits" (levels) of careers to guide the student's choice of course work. For example, in the environmental, physical sciences, and health sciences fields, careers (such as those in Table 4.2) are listed for the students' reference.

Orbit 1 requires a high school credential plus up to six months of additional training. Orbit 2 requires up to two years of additional

Table 4.2. Orbits for Environmental, Physical, and Life Sciences
—David Douglas High School

Orbit 1	Orbit 2	Orbit 3
Commercial fisherman	Animal caretaker	Astronomer
Farm and ranch hand	Dental lab technician	Biologist
Forest conservation worker	Fish, wildlife technician	Environmentalist
Floral designer	Farmer, rancher	Dentist
Garbage collector	Forestry technician	Forester
Gardener	Licensed practical nurse	Geologist
Home health aide	Medical lab technician	Physician
Nursing center aide	Microcomputer computer specialist	Veterinarian
Recycler	Optician	Oceanographer

SOURCE: David Douglas High School, Portland, Oregon; used by permission.

training or education; and orbit 3 requires four or more years of college in addition to high school. Students plan the four-year high school program after exploring career options and aptitudes in grades 7 and 8. They may change their career paths in high school if they wish to select a new direction.

Teachers, counselors, administrators, and three to five business partners are formed into interdisciplinary teams within each career constellation. The team establishes curriculum, sets policy, and determines how to provide the best program for students. They design curriculum and lessons to have students apply the concepts, principles, and processes of the academic curriculum in a career-related context. In addition to the application of learning in classroom simulations of career tasks, students have opportunities to take part in job shadowing, internships, and work experience.

The Oregon Education Act (House Bill 3565) contains legislation establishing the educational performance standards for all students to be attained by the 10th grade (Certificate of Initial Mastery). This act also requires that students earn a Certificate of Advanced Mastery by the end of the 12th grade endorsing them in at least one of six broad career fields. Legislation dealing with "school to work transition" is developing in state governments and departments of education across the country. The federal government is also working on legislation to further states' efforts. Funding will flow to those who develop promising programs to raise academic and performance standards to ensure a globally competitive workforce.

The Arizona Model for Vocational Technological Education

Since 1988, the Arizona Department of Education has been working on the restructuring of vocational technological education. This effort has involved the three state universities, many local school districts, and business and industry partners. Arizona vocational technological education is continually evolving toward a vision of high technical and academic competence.

The Arizona model provides four levels of instruction that begin in the seventh grade with a broad overview of occupations and development of core technical skills. The learning continues through postsecondary programs with increasing occupational specialization of knowledge and skills.

The four levels of sequenced instruction are integrated through six strands of developmental outcomes. The strands in the Arizona model (Arizona Department of Education, 1992) are as follows:

- *Thinking Skills*—including decision making, problem solving, creativity, and dealing with change
- *Career Development Skills*—including career exploration, career decision making, and job acquisition skills
- *Applied Academic Skills*—including communication, mathematics, and science related to technical areas
- *Life Management Skills*—including interpersonal relationships, wellness, group processes, health, and safety
- *Business, Economic, and Leadership Skills*—including business economics, entrepreneurship, marketing procedures, and continuous improvement processes

---

Level 1—Technological Exploration and Foundations

THINKING SKILLS
- Describe the processes of decision making and problem solving
- Compare and contrast different decision-making and problem-solving skills
- Define and demonstrate how one acquires information
- Define a variety of creative thinking skills
- Describe the effects of change

CAREER DEVELOPMENT SKILLS
- Describe and demonstrate school and work ethics
- Identify and explore areas of career interest
- Experience meaningful and relevant activities related to areas of interest
- Explore occupational cluster choices

APPLIED ACADEMIC SKILLS
- Identify and demonstrate basic academic skills
- Describe the relationship between academic skills and occupational skills
- Identify careers that capitalize on specific academic strengths and interests

LIFE MANAGEMENT SKILLS
- Identify characteristics of effective interpersonal relationships
- Identify wellness, health, and safety concepts
- Identify personal, economic, and environmental resources
- Define self-concept and identify self-esteem issues
- Identify and explore group processes
- Perform effectively as an individual and member of a team

BUSINESS, ECONOMIC, AND LEADERSHIP SKILLS
- Describe basic economic concepts and systems
- Describe the characteristics of a successful business
- Describe the value of work to the individual, community, and nation
- Identify qualities and types of leaders
- Define and describe cultural diversity
- Explain the value of continually improving the work process

TECHNOLOGY SKILLS
- Describe and demonstrate basic technological principles and processes
- Demonstrate basic computer skills

Figure 4.15. Arizona Model—Preliminary Strand Outcomes (Interim Design Report, July 1992)
SOURCE: Arizona Department of Education; used by permission.

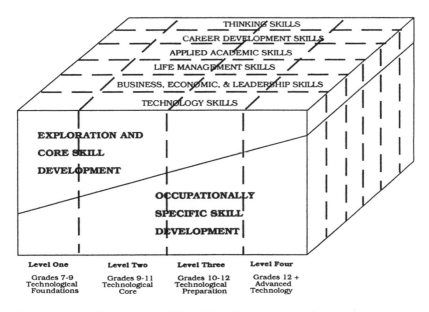

THINKING SKILLS

CAREER DEVELOPMENT SKILLS

APPLIED ACADEMIC SKILLS

LIFE MANAGEMENT SKILLS

BUSINESS, ECONOMIC, & LEADERSHIP SKILLS

TECHNOLOGY SKILLS

EXPLORATION AND

CORE SKILL

DEVELOPMENT

OCCUPATIONALLY

SPECIFIC SKILL

DEVELOPMENT

Level One	**Level Two**	**Level Three**	**Level Four**
Grades 7-9 Technological Foundations	Grades 9-11 Technological Core	Grades 10-12 Technological Preparation	Grades 12 + Advanced Technology

Figure 4.16. The Arizona Model for Vocational Technological Education (Interim Design Report, July 1992)
SOURCE: Arizona Department of Education; used by permission.

- *Technology Skills*—including computer skills and applications of new and advanced technologies

Each strand is defined by developmental outcomes as shown in Figure 4.15.

The Arizona model is depicted in Figure 4.16. As students progress from level one to level four, they move from the exploratory study of occupations and the development of basic work skills to specific occupational skill development and experience with advanced technologies. The outcome strands are woven throughout the academic and career curriculum and develop increasing sophistication as students progress through the grades.

The curriculum framework for level one was developed by the staff of Arizona State University for 17 sites, predominantly junior high and middle schools, during the 1991-1992 school year. The

Theme A—Communicating Information

1.0 Students will gather, interpret, and evaluate information
1.1   Apply a decision-making/problem-solving strategy
1.2   Practice working in groups
1.3   Locate information sources
1.4   Match personal aptitudes and interests to courses of study
1.5   Explore careers in communication
1.6   Develop an awareness of career information resources
1.7   Verify the reliability and accuracy of information
1.8   Apply comprehensive strategies
1.9   Apply ethics in reporting and using information
1.10 Discuss similarities between class/school rules and work rules

Theme B—Explaining Energy/Matter and Machines

1.0 Students will identify types of energy and their physical properties
1.1   Explain potential energy
1.2   Discuss the role of motion in kinetic energy
1.3   Identify the properties and uses of magnetism
1.4   Demonstrate the effect of friction on machines
1.5   Use temperature to control matter
1.6   Use light and color to alter matter

2.0 Students will understand the transfer of energy to power
2.1   Explain the use of air, fluid, and electricity in a power system
2.2   Use standard measurement abbreviations and equivalents
2.3   Use measuring and timing devices
2.4   Evaluate ethical implications of decisions about energy

Figure 4.17. Arizona Model: Level 1 Competencies and
Competency (Sample) Indicators (Interim Design Report, July 1992)
SOURCE: Arizona Department of Education; used by permission.

framework identifies skills and concepts that cut across occupations,
and organizes content according to the following themes:

- Communicating information
- Explaining energy, matter, and machines
- Relating technology and science
- Producing and processing

The themes are delineated further by specific competencies and competency-based indicators (see Figure 4.17).

Career Path Curriculum Design

The blending of a traditional liberal arts, college preparation program in high schools and a career path model presents major curricular design questions:

- How can we preserve the integrity of a liberal arts philosophy and at the same time provide a school program that prepares students for work as well as for further education?
- How can we develop the high-level performance skills outlined in the SCANS report through an integrated academic and vocational curriculum?

Though I usually advocate making change in incremental steps, beginning with what is and then moving forward as people appear ready in knowledge and desire, I hold a different view for high school restructuring. We have become complacently inured with the two-track model of vocational and college preparation programs in our high schools. We have been squeezing too many students through the cookie tube, ill-prepared for either work or college.

Our traditional high school curriculum is delivered as if all students, except those we funnel into vocational education, will graduate from a four-year college. And unlike countries such as Germany or Japan, we have denigrated vocational education as less worthy than the college preparatory program. Yet the statistics show that only 30% to 40% of students go on to university programs. Where is our conscience for the other 60%? And even those who go on to complete college have traditionally had little experience with the kinds of skills outlined in SCANS.

We will never break down these barriers between the perceived academic and vocational tracks by minor tinkering. We need to design entirely new models for high schools, such as the career path models, that design integrated curricular programs to meet outcomes drawn from at least three sources:

- SCANS—to meet the needs of a quality workforce
- The aims of liberal arts curricula—to preserve the lessons of discourse, culture, and humanity
- Life skill curricula—to be prepared for daily living

A danger with career path models is that the liberal arts and life skill curricula will be lost in the preparation of future workers. But in spite of this possibility, we must alter the traditional program to bring contemporary relevance and meaning to each student's education. I believe the dangers can be avoided with thoughtful curricular planning and multiple source outcomes as stated previously.

Once the multiple source outcomes and performance indicators are defined for the school program, two different approaches to curriculum design seem appropriate.

In the first approach, key concepts related to the subject areas that support the particular career path are identified. In a career path titled "Environmental, Physical, and Health Sciences," examples of key concepts might be "Sustainability," "Deforestation," or "Pollution" for the environment; "Force," "Cause/Effect," or "Quantification" for physical science; or "Model," "Disease," or "Organism" for health sciences. With this approach, the content can be defined as topics related to the different concepts through the grade levels. Concepts can be repeated through the grades with developing sophistication of the related topical themes and essential learnings. New concepts can also be added as the curriculum becomes more complex.

For interdisciplinary units, what might be a narrow topic within a subject area study (e.g., "Machines as an example of force" in physical science) is developed into a broader, interdisciplinary, topical theme that draws from the different disciplines. An example of a broader, interdisciplinary theme linked to the concept of *Force* might be as follows: "How is 'force' used to facilitate work in different occupations: oceanographer? forester? chemist? radiology technician? recycler?"

The topical theme is related to the concept under study across the disciplines so that learning moves beyond low-level fact study. Remember that it is the concept that draws thinking to the analysis and synthesis levels. It is also helpful to phrase the topical theme in the form of a question, problem, or issue to send the students on a quest for knowledge and to motivate curiosity.

As process subjects, English and mathematics are applied across the interdisciplinary fields of study. All teachers are teachers of language, and mathematics extends understanding across disciplines. Both subjects communicate meaning. The skills of English and mathematics can be taught in single subject study, but they gain meaning and practicality in authentic life contexts. The addition of courses such as "Journalistic English" help set an instructional stage for the application of writing and English skills in a real-world context.

The second method for designing curriculum for career paths maintains the traditional subjects and encourages teachers to make connections to the vocations and the vocational content of the career path. I would call this a coordinated curriculum approach rather than an integrated one, because the curriculum depends on connections to vocations rather than the integration of academic and vocational education under common concepts and themes.

Significant high school change will require extensive dialogue between academic and vocational teachers, administrators, parents, and the business community. It will be important for all parties to see the perceived need and to agree that things must change. How that change occurs will require teamwork, the ability to leave the familiar in curriculum and instruction, and the willingness to take some risks. Teachers will need to feel that the risks are supported by administrators and parents. The business community must take a partnership role in helping to suggest and design "authentic" experiences or simulations for students. Schools can gain suggestions for classroom simulations by surveying local businesses for a list of employee activities that require the use of the various SCANS competencies. The survey describes the competencies and leaves room for the employer (or employees) to fill in related job responsibilities and tasks. These can then be transformed into classroom simulations by the teachers.

Florida's School-to-Work Continuum

For the past six years, the state of Florida has been operating from its *Blueprint for Career Preparation* (1989) to provide a quality workforce. Vocational programs are being developed and refined according to the competencies outlined by the Secretary's Commission on Achieving Necessary Skills (SCANS), which were outlined in Chapter 2 of this book. A variety of programs and incentives make up the school-to-work continuum from elementary through postsecondary school.

One example, the Quad County Tech Prep Program, is a cooperative partnership between the community college, the school districts, and local business leaders. More than 1,000 teachers have been trained in coordinating and integrating academic and technical content. At the high school level, the academic core uses applied academics and develops technical skills in the four curriculum clusters: Industrial Technology, Business Management, Allied Health, and Agritechnology.

Educational summits are held yearly to provide feedback and suggestions from the 200-plus businesses in the county. Business leaders are included in the design and delivery of curriculum and staff development training as well. Students can earn college credits in high school through the Tech Prep Program, and community colleges are developing applied academics programs to extend training for students after high school.

National Center for
Research in Vocational Education

In *New Designs for the Comprehensive High School*, Copa and Pease (1992) document an extensive review of past and current research, designs, and theories related to curriculum, instruction, and assessment for the American high school. Based on this review and on discussions related to the need for change, a national design group composed of high school and university instructors, leaders, and board members, as well as business executives, brought together leading specifications for all aspects of high school design.

Finding that the traditional high school design impedes integrated and cooperative learning processes, the design group developed examples of comprehensive designs for use by schools and school districts about to transform existing schools or build new ones. The project also addresses specifications for learner outcomes; curriculum, instruction, and assessment; school organization and business/community partnerships; staffing and staff development; and construction costs.

The *New Design* curriculum specifications are not outlined in detail, but they do call for the integration of vocational and academic education focused on the attainment of high-level student outcomes. Educators are encouraged to make full use of community sites in addition to the school building and to design structured work experiences for students.

The learning specifications of the *New Design* project limit groupings of students in large schools. Design models show learning environments for groups of 250-500 students, with personal workstations for groups of 5 students.

I recommend *New Designs for the Comprehensive High School* as an excellent resource for stimulating discussion and for planning new models and approaches for a tired tradition.

It is critical that our traditional high school structure, organization, and pedagogical practices are rapidly changed. Involving students in meaningful, applied curriculum that develops their life skills, motivates their mind, and engages their spirit will brighten a fading light. All students deserve a quality education. We must fix the problems of slip in, slide through, or shoved out.

The programs that effectively blend vocational and academic curriculum, and structure learning toward high-level outcomes such as those outlined in the SCANS report, offer promising models for secondary schools.

At the same time, we have to balance a curriculum that prepares students for work, citizenship, and family life with a curriculum that

- ensures success in further schooling,
- develops aesthetic knowledge and appreciation, and
- develops healthy self-esteem, values, and ethics.

It is for this reason that I advocate defining the major concepts and critical content that underlie the separate academic and vocational subject areas prior to integrating content. Concepts that cut across disciplines can then serve to integrate the content. The focus of content can be defined through the unit themes. Themes should be centered on significant issues, problems, or questions related to humanity and our world in all of its complexity. Themes are drawn from all contexts of life including work, family, aesthetics, sport, health and well-being, and political, economic, and sociocultural issues. Even if a school has a career path focus, the themes of study need to include the range of life issues to develop a balanced foundation of knowledge, skills, attitudes, and values.

SUMMARY

An interdisciplinary, integrated curriculum takes the thinking process to the levels of analysis, synthesis, and evaluation. It is to be used as one form of curriculum design that helps students understand major concepts, themes, problems, or issues from multiple perspectives.

Integrated, interdisciplinary curricula differ from coordinated, multidisciplinary curricula in cognitive sophistication. To be integrated and interdisciplinary, there must be a conceptual focus for the study that takes thinking beyond the factual level. The common conceptual focus creates the integrated perspective.

Multidisciplinary curricula are coordinated to a lower level topic, such as "Trees," or "South America," and are fact and activity focused. Teachers often begin their journey toward integrated curricula at this level.

Teachers at all levels are experimenting with integrated curricula. Perhaps the most complex integrated programs today are being developed in the theme-based high schools, such as the career path or academy models.

Though interdisciplinary, integrated curricula offer many benefits to the educational program, they should not totally replace the discipline-based fields of study. There are many questions that remain to be answered before we are ready to make that move. We can combine fields of study into broader discipline categories, such as arts and humanities, but we need to maintain the integrity of the critical, discipline-based concepts, content, and ways of thinking.

Extending Thought

1. Take one subject area such as science or art. Can you identify five of the major organizing concepts for that discipline? How do you know the terms you have chosen are concepts?
2. Define some of the topics that you consider to be "critical content" for the concepts you identified in question 1. How did you determine that the content is "critical"? Is it critical for the 21st century?
3. What criteria can we use to determine if content is critical for the 21st century?
4. What value does concept-based curriculum design have over topically based curriculum design in terms of the following:

   – reducing the overloaded content curriculum,
   – focusing instruction to facilitate higher order thinking,
   – integrating content curriculum,
   – sharing the commonality as well as the diversity of culture and humanity, and
   – highlighting the lessons of history through time?

5. How can teachers involve students in the design of integrated units?
6. React to this statement: "Teachers do not need to know all of the specific content information of a unit prior to student engagement. They learn along with the students who search out and construct knowledge. Teachers do, however, need to think through the anticipated interplay of theme, concept, and topics to determine some of the key generalizations, or transferable learnings, that they expect students to derive."
7. Discuss the dilemma at the high school level between providing a traditional college preparatory curriculum and a work pre-

paratory curriculum. How can both aims be accommodated through an integrated curricular program that will alleviate the traditional view of academics versus vocational training.

8. Considering Reich's four basic skills of the valued "Symbolic Analyst"—abstraction, system thinking, experimentation, and collaboration—compare a lecture/textbook approach to instruction and an integrated, interdisciplinary approach. Which instructional approach would best facilitate the development of each skill? How?

9. Consider the implications of the evolving definition of *Depth of Instruction:*

   – *Depth of Instruction* used to mean "teaching more facts about a single topic."

   – *Depth of Instruction* today means "teaching higher level thinking related to a significant concept and theme, problem, or issue by connecting ideas across disciplines to extend understanding, find answers, foster generalizations, and create new knowledge."

CHAPTER 5

Assessing and Reporting Student Progress

T he choke hold that standardized, normative-referenced tests have had on teaching and learning for the past 30 years has been relaxed, though not eliminated. The demand for assessment measures that accurately describe what students can do—in addition to what they know—has loosened slightly the fingers of narrowness, shallowness, bias, inequity, and gotcha!

Although we rejoice at the trend to relax the grip of standardized tests, we must maintain a keen eye on the developing national and state performance assessments. Subject area committees at the national and state levels are busy outlining content and performance standards that hint, suspiciously, at familiar high-stakes, comparative evaluation and at times overkill.

In some cases, the state and national standards are helpful because they are broad frameworks showing the critical concepts, salient principles, and desired performances for a discipline. In other cases, the standards are a rewrite of specific content objectives from the early 1980s, with the add-ons of expected performance outcomes. In too many cases, the standards are being implemented with "high-stakes" legislation. Students will be denied a high school diploma if the standards are not demonstrated in the complex tests. The choke hold returns.

There are policymakers who seem to have nine lives. They appear in each generation with the persuasive argument that, if we just test for what we want, the product will emerge. The testing machine will magically transform instruction to the identified ends. It is true that defining the targets for curriculum and instruction in the assessment instruments will *assist* in making changes in the classroom. But to assume that an instructional change from a fact-based to a process-based teaching emphasis will occur without systematic staff development is short-circuited thinking. It is like sending people on a journey to a distant destination with only a few sketchy examples showing the general direction toward the end point. The map and supplies for survival are lost in the dust.

We can, and should, set performance standards, and monitor and adjust curriculum and instruction from elementary through secondary school to ensure that each child reaches the graduating standards—but *mastery* is a misnomer in process development. The road to mastery is a lifelong journey.

Teachers and performance assessment specialists will need to continue their partnership in developing a rational approach to measuring what students know and can do related to significant schooling outcomes. They are in a race with irrational expectations in many states—high-stakes cognitive and performance standards applied to bulging curricula with inadequate attention to the need for teacher and administrator training, professional dialogue, and student support. Without this focus at the teaching level, the testing mandates are going to swing around and knock the policymakers off their feet.

Parents will not stand for their students being held back from graduation. The resulting dialogue will highlight the conditions of inequity and the needs for instructional and student support. Why wait for this hailstorm to occur? Why not develop a reasonable "systems" approach for addressing the desired student outcomes? Rather than a simplistic, top-down, "test is best" mentality, we should evaluate the foundation for learning at the classroom level and weigh instructional practices and student needs against the desired subject area standards and graduation outcomes.

Each component of the school system—curriculum, instruction, evaluation and assessment, decision making, leadership, roles, communication, human resource development, parents, and community—should be evaluated and aligned toward the achievement of success for all students as defined by desired outcomes and standards. Some school districts have shown foresight and are taking such a systems approach to restructuring.

In this chapter, we will focus on the component of evaluation and assessment, beginning with a brief comparison of normative- referenced, criterion-referenced, and performance-based measures. Then we will take a closer look at process and performance assessments by studying specific classroom examples. Key to the discussion will be the critical importance of student self-assessment. The value of "authentic" assessment as a means of relating learning to real-life contexts and situations will be displayed through selected examples. Steps for designing performance assessments to evaluate the unit outcome and activity for integrated units of instruction will lead into a summary discussion on the value of performance-based measurement.

A Brief Review:
Form and Function

Normative-Referenced Tests

Normative-referenced tests are designed to assess and compare mass populations on specific items of knowledge or skill. They can be multiple choice and machine-scored instruments. When these tests are used to place a student or a group of students in rank order compared with other test takers in the same grade or age population, the test is normatively referenced. Normative-referenced, standardized tests were influenced heavily by the use of a multiple choice format on the Army Alpha examination during World War I. The Alpha format efficiently and effectively sorted nearly 2 million military personnel to determine aptitude for officer status (Popham, 1993).

Criterion-Referenced Tests

Criterion-referenced tests became especially popular in the late 1970s and 1980s as an attempt to identify clearly and specifically what knowledge and skills students are to master. Criterion-referenced tests measure the objectives taught in the classroom. They intend to highlight a student's strengths and weaknesses. Because of their close alignment to the curriculum, it has been traditionally assumed that remediating the test areas would achieve student success.

According to James Popham, however, weak test design—focused too often on "skill and drill" instruction—has impeded the potential of quality criterion-referenced tests. Popham states that we need to promote "generalizable" mastery of skills. This can be accomplished through criterion-referenced tests that focus on the intellectual skills required by the testing task and that provide a variety of assessment tactics (Popham, 1993). We will return to the issue of "generalizability" of assessment results later in this chapter.

Alternative Assessments

Alternative assessments is a catchphrase for a renewed look at forms of assessment that depart from the traditional multiple choice, nor- matively referenced tests. The Outcomes movement raised questions with the testing establishment concerning the usefulness of stand- ardized tests in sharing information on what students are actually capable of "doing." In response to the many questions, and to meet the changing emphases in assessment, alternative forms of assess- ment are being designed. Many alternative assessments require stu- dents to "construct" or create responses rather than to simply react or respond to given statements or conditions. Different forms of alternative assessment emphasize a specific focus.

Performance assessments combine content and process into a format that shows what students know—and what they can do with what they know. Performance assessments take knowledge to the doing level. The assessments may be authentic, as defined below, but are not always so. Performance assessments often take traditional con- tent, such as information on the Civil War, and engage students in a performance task calling on knowledge and skills. The performance might be an essay or an exhibition such as a play, a debate, or a visual representation.

Portfolio assessment emphasizes student self-assessment. A portfolio is a collection of student work that tells a story through time. It shows growth and development related to established criteria. The purpose of a portfolio is to facilitate classroom learning and instruction.

Authentic assessment is based on meaningful performances that are drawn from "real-world" contexts. The assessments are simulations of problems, issues, or challenges that a professional worker or adult might face in his or her life.

Alternative assessments support the recognized need to develop the internal process, or lifelong learning skills, of each child. Assessment of individual, developing "performance" comes into balance with developing concept/content understanding in instruction and assessment.

Developmental Process Assessments

The alternative assessments discussed in the preceding section measure both process and content. But they are often only "snapshots" of a student's performance in time.

To effectively monitor a student's continuous development within each process area from primary grades through high school, we need to identify the developmental characteristics or indicators for each developmental stage. The developmental stages may be defined by grade bands, such as K-2, 3-4, 5-6, or by individual grade designations with a range of indicators. The developmental indicators are grouped under organizing categories. For example, the process area of writing could be defined by the categories of *organization, mechanics, style,* and *development of ideas.*

Specific indicators for beginning, intermediate, and advanced performance provide teachers with a developmental road map for helping students celebrate how far they have come and for showing the next steps. Figure 5.1 provides an example of writing indicators from the fourth-grade level in a K-12 sequence of developmental

150

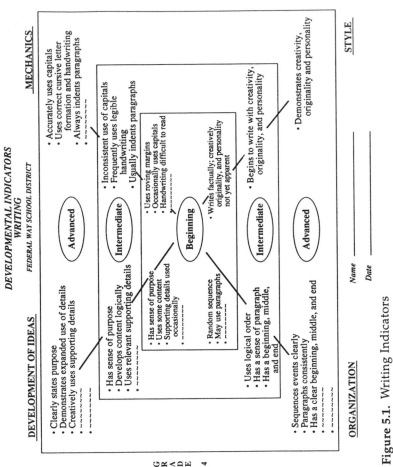

Figure 5.1. Writing Indicators

SOURCE: Federal Way Public Schools, Federal Way, Washington; used by permission.

indicators from the Federal Way, Washington, School District. These indicators are used in an ongoing assessment of student work, which is collected over time in individual writing folios.

Many school districts have developed indicators for writing, reading, and speaking. The most authentic indicators are those that are drawn from the actual performance of students in the district. In Federal Way, the writing indicators were developed by a large teacher committee that examined hundreds of samples of student writing, K-12, to identify the salient developmental indicators for each category.

It is important to develop a folio of exemplar papers for each grade band. These papers provide teachers with concrete examples, or benchmarks, of beginning, intermediate, and advanced work in each category. Critical to quality assessment is teacher training on how to assess papers according to the identified criteria and standards.

The Implications of Process Assessment

Process and content are two different entities. Process skills develop internally within each child; content is inert and exists outside of the child. Because of these differences, we should teach and assess process and content in different ways. But, traditionally, we have treated them alike. We have called the processes of reading and writing "subjects." We have graded students in these "subjects" using a deficit model of grading—harping on what they cannot yet do rather than celebrating their accomplishments and showing them the path to the next stage of development. I believe this deficit approach to process development is one reason that so many children feel defeated by third grade.

Two examples illustrate the deficit model for grading process development. The first example is from Federal Way, Washington. When the teachers in Federal Way reviewed their first draft of the writing indicators K-12, they realized that the writing indicators for the advanced level students were all affirmative statements: "Clearly states purpose," "Creatively uses supporting details," "Demonstrates personality," and so on, but the beginning level used overwhelmingly negative statements: "No purpose shown," "Lacks supporting details," "Lacks personality," and so on.

The teachers recognized that this approach to writing assessment, which rightfully measures a student against a set standard, broke down at the beginning levels. A deficit model took over at this level, defining what students could not do rather than defining the developmental capabilities that were demonstrated in the beginning stages of writing for their age range. Teachers realized how defeating the negative assessments were to a child. How many of us would want to go to work and be told, day in and day out, what we cannot do in our performance? Wouldn't we achieve greater growth by knowing how much positive gain we were making toward the standard?

The teachers took the first draft and reframed the question for students in the beginning developmental levels of writing: "What abilities *are* demonstrated by our students at each developmental stage as they work toward the standard?" This was difficult because it meant task analyzing to define the indicators of success at the beginning developmental levels of the writing process. The discussion among the teachers was invaluable, however, as they began to look at their students as developing rather than as deficit learners. Conceptually, they started to view each learner as being on a positive learning curve rather than being a plus or minus point on a bell-shaped curve.

The second example of a deficit assessment mode relates to the measurement of graduation outcomes. Some districts have developed qualitative scales to assess individual performance for outcomes such as "Collaborative Contributor." The highest level of the scale describes the Collaborative Contributor with positive indicators such as "Task oriented," "Monitors own behavior to facilitate the work of the group," "Contributes ideas thoughtfully," and so on. The lowest level of the scale describes the student's performance in deficit terms: "Off-task," "Does not monitor behavior to support group," "Disrupts group process."

If we believe that the ability to collaborate is a developmental process, then we have to wonder why we assess the student's progress as if he or she should already have arrived—no matter what the age or developmental level. Would we use such a deficit model to encourage a 1-year-old to walk or a 2-year-old to talk? Teaching for process development in the school-age child requires the same kind of praise, encouragement, and support that we provide the preschool child who is learning to talk, walk, think, and speak. Assessment scales need to be supportive of learning at all levels rather than negatively evaluative of students at the beginning levels.

The deficit model of assessment is apparent in most performance-based rubrics today. Are we really measuring "progress" toward a standard if we give no credit at the beginning levels for what students can do in relation to the standard? What effect does negative feedback have on the developing processes that are so sensitively related to the child's ego and personal being? Highly successful coaches set and clarify the standard for athletes—but they positively celebrate small advancements toward the goal. Corrections are made but expressed belief in the individual, and support through the different levels of development, are the main strategies for training.

Reporting Process Development

As a result of the renewed perspective that language is a developing process, the Federal Way Public Schools have revised their elementary report card. Student progress in writing is placed along a developmental continuum at a beginning, intermediate, or advanced level in kindergarten through sixth grade. The goal is to place all language skills on a developmental continuum on the report card and remove the meaningless letter grades. Each parent receives a booklet showing all of the Writing Indicators K-12 when a child enters school. Parents are encouraged to follow and assist their child's progress.

Report cards that give a letter grade for reading, writing, oral communication, or any other developing process skill do not provide a helpful profile for what the child has actually accomplished. Narrative reports that detail the child's progress through descriptive indicators of actual performance are far more meaningful to both parents and child. These reports become even more valuable when the child has self-assessed his or her own work according to defined performance indicators.

In the Federal Way School District, and many other districts around the country, teachers are providing students with Develop-

mental Writing Indicators such as those shown in Figure 5.1. They
ask the students to self-assess their writing and provide written reactions before turning their work in to the teacher. Peer assessment is often
a step in the writing process. There has been a great deal written in
the literature concerning the benefits of both peer assessment and
student self-assessment and critique. I believe self-assessment, especially, is a critical practice to help students take more responsibility
for their learning and to encourage a standard of high-quality work.

Wang, Haertel, and Walberg (1993), in a *Review of Educational
Research* article titled "Toward a Knowledge Base for School Learning," present the results of a comprehensive meta-analysis of factors influencing the teaching and learning process as drawn from
quantitative research syntheses, summaries by educational experts,
and narrative reviews representing thousands of statistical relations. Though the journal also contains review articles that question
the feasibility of generalizing the conditions for teaching and learning from rules formed by researchers who are removed from the
context of the classroom (Kleibard, 1993), I feel the results deserve
consideration.

According to the authors, the categories having the most influence
on student learning, as shown through the meta-analysis, were these:

- Classroom management
- Metacognitive (the student's ability to self-assess)
- Cognitive (general intelligence, prior knowledge, specific con-
  tent knowledge, as well as motivational and affective attributes
  such as perseverance and enthusiasm for learning)
- Home environment and parental support
- Student and teacher social interactions (Wang et al., 1993)

The findings show that "proximal" variables, those close to the
student such as *psychological, home environment,* and *instructional*
variables, have strong influence on school learning. "Distal" variables, or variables that are farther removed from the student, such as
state and district policies or student demographic characteristics,
have less of an impact on learning (Wang et al., 1993).

This analysis is in alignment with current beliefs and trends in education. Though we have always been concerned with classroom management as an issue, the question today is how to manage a classroom so that the cognitive and metacognitive structures are facilitated to maximize learning. Thinking students and thinking teachers take greater responsibility for their work and function at increasingly sophisticated levels of performance.

Schools are vitally concerned with bringing parents in as partners in the educational process. This concern coincides with the findings by Wang et al. that home environment and parental support are critical to the educational success of children. All of the performance assessment in the world will not bring success to a suicidal child who is verbally or physically abused.

And, finally, teachers have always known, but sometimes need to be reminded, that the interpersonal interaction with each of their students has a significant impact on their students' success. Students look to their teacher for acceptance and support. We need to value all children, talk and connect with them, and show interest in their growth and development in learning.

Assessing Critical Thinking Developmentally

Critical thinking is one of the most challenging areas to be assessed as a developmental process. It is challenging because there are few models that define indicators of developing sophistication for this area. There have been some benchmark "snapshots" that describe critical thinking in a general way as applied to a specific task, but we need a more complete picture to assist teachers.

There is no question that the development of sophisticated thinking abilities is required for individual success in the 21st century. National, state, and district outcomes specify the ability to think critically, problem solve, and reason as key goals for education. But teachers have had little training in how to teach for, and assess, thinking abilities. This is a more serious problem than most policymakers recognize. Teachers know this is a critical area of need for staff development.

In addition to the limited emphasis on this area in teacher training programs, our traditional curriculum fosters the antithesis of higher order thinking. A primary focus on kings, queens, and dates, isolated mathematical algorithms, grammar drills, and the memorization of isolated fact after fact hinders the pursuit of higher order understandings. Lower order memory work should not be the end of instruction. It should be viewed as a necessary tool for effective higher order thinking.

The past decade spawned a variety of programs intended to teach for transfer of thinking. Many of these programs were add-on thinking skill exercises that took anywhere from 15 to 60 instructional minutes per day. The goal was transferability of the thinking skill into the regular work with curriculum.

Today, however, the trend is away from isolated thinking skill instruction to embedded thinking as a natural part of the teaching/ learning process. So the question remains, "How can we identify the developmental indicators of critical thinking to facilitate the progress of each child as he or she moves through the grades?"

Standards for Thinking

We can find help in answering the question by starting with seven of the standards for critical thinking that have been identified by Richard Paul at the Center for Critical Thinking, Sonoma State University.

Paul states, and rightly so, that it is not enough only to analyze or evaluate material. We must apply a set of standards to specify the quality of analysis or evaluation that is performed.

Seven of the fourteen intellectual standards identified by Paul (1993a) are as follows:

- Clarity
- Depth
- Accuracy
- Breadth

- Precision
- Significance
- Relevance

To maintain coherence with the terminology used in this chapter, we will substitute the word *traits* for Paul's *standards* because we define a *trait* as a characteristic or quality to be evaluated and the *standard* as the set point for quality performance.

To help students learn how to think critically, we need to define the indicators for each of these traits. What does *clarity* "look like" at grades K-2? 3-5? 6-8? 9-12? We could say that "clarity is clarity" no matter what the grade level. This is true. Clarity is a concept with the attributes of "clearness" and "lucidity," no matter what the grade level. So when we begin to assess what the critical thinking traits look like at each grade band, we have to go beyond the simple, generalizable attributes.

We need to consider how clarity will be expressed as applied to particular content. The expression of clarity as a *developmental performance* is dependent on a number of factors:

- The sophistication of the content in terms of depth and complexity of ideas
- The cognitive processing of the student—his or her ability to analyze, synthesize, and organize content and ideas
- The communication ability of the student—his or her skill in conveying ideas so that others clearly understand the message

Let's examine a specific case where increasing sophistication of content provides a framework for assessing developing sophistication in critical thinking processes.

In Chapter 3, I discussed the idea of organizing a social studies curriculum according to a limited number of organizing concepts that cut through all grades K-6. The expanding themes at each grade level are considered in relation to the organizing concept of "Interdependence" for the instructional unit. The theme of "Families and Interdependence" at grades K-1 leads to increasingly sophisticated themes: "Communities and Interdependence," "States and Interdependence," "Interdependence in Our Nation," and "Interdependence in Our World." Content is "nested" under these increasingly sophisticated conceptual themes.

As students participate in many activities related to the theme of study, they will develop increasingly sophisticated generalizations to parallel the depth of the content study. Remember that a universal generalization is two or more concepts stated in a relationship that holds through time. So a child arrives inductively at increasingly sophisticated generalizations related to the concept of "Interdependence" at the various grade levels:

- Grade 1: A family cares for its members.
- Grade 3: A community provides for needs and wants.
- Grade 5: A society is socially and economically interdependent.
- Grade 6: World cultures vary in their economic dependence on trade.

A teacher might provide students with one or more generalizations at the end of a learning unit and ask the students to give examples and defend or refute the generalization based on the unit study and additional student-generated examples. The teacher states that "clarity" will be one of the traits by which the presentation is judged. The product can be oral, written, or visual, but all of the expected traits and criteria for assessment are made clear to the student at the beginning of the unit work.

How will we let third graders know what clarity looks like? How about our fifth or sixth graders? Students can participate in developing the indicators of a trait. Along with a discussion of the trait, students need to see and discuss actual examples of clear presentations. They need to self-assess their own work for clarity.

As learners progress through the grades, the standard for clarity challenges ability. Students organize and express increasingly sophisticated content. They also have to explain in a self-assessment how their work has met, or is developing toward, the standard performance. Helping students to define the meaning and standard expectations for a trait, and challenging students to reach the standard with increasingly complex material, will be a big step forward for education. Even though we analyze and evaluate with abandon in education, traditional instruction has failed to consistently hold students to progressive intellectual standards.

The Elements of Reasoning

Paul discusses the importance of considering the *elements of reasoning* when evaluating students' critical thinking processes. Paul (1993b) defines the elements of reasoning as "the basic conditions implicit whenever we gather, conceptualize, apply, analyze, synthesize, or evaluate information" (p. 154). We must evaluate whether or not the student is using the elements of reasoning and apply the intellectual standards (traits) to his or her thought process. Paul's (1993b) elements of reasoning are summarized briefly:

1. *Purpose, goal, or end in view:* To what end goal, or purpose, is the reasoning focused?
2. *Question at issue, or problem to be solved:* Has the question at issue, or the problem, been clearly formulated?
3. *Point of view, or frame of reference:* The student's point of view should adhere to the relevant intellectual standards. It may be broad, flexible, fair, and clearly stated, for example.
4. *The empirical dimension of reasoning:* Students receive feedback on their ability to give evidence that is gathered and reported clearly, fairly, and accurately. The empirical data are measured against the standards.
5. *The conceptual dimension of reasoning:* Any defect in the concepts or ideas of the reasoning is a possible source of problems in student reasoning. Are concepts and ideas clear and relevant to the issue?
6. *Assumptions:* The students' assumptions are measured against the standards. Are the assumptions justifiable? Clear? Crucial or extraneous?
7. *Implications and consequences:* Students need help in internalizing both the relevant standards for reasoning out implications (and consequences) and the degree to which their own reasoning meets those standards.
8. *Inferences:* Assessment would evaluate a student's ability to make sound inferences in his or her reasoning. When is an inference sound? Are the inferences clear? Justifiable? Do they draw deep conclusions or do they stick to the trivial and superficial?

Generalizability

An issue of concern in performance assessment relates to the generalizability of test results related to the content under scrutiny. Just because a student demonstrates content knowledge related to the Westward Movement, for example, does not ensure that the student will demonstrate content knowledge related to any other topic in American history. Generalizability of knowledge is not guaranteed.

Because of this problem, some assessment specialists (Baker, 1994; Popham, 1993) recommend that the assessment focus be placed on the generalizable process skill. Their reasoning is that assessment results of specific content knowledge are not generalizable, but process abilities do generalize. We apply common process skills across content fields. Therefore the results of process skill assessments are generalizable. Critical thinking is an example of a generalizable process skill.

This approach acknowledges the importance of assessing process skill, but it still leaves two questions.

Can we assume that process performance is generalizable? Process performance—how well a student reads, writes, speaks, thinks, or performs—is directly correlated to the degree of conceptual difficulty presented by the assessment task. The process performance is only generalizable to tasks of comparable conceptual difficulty.

Is it possible to generalize content knowledge and understanding beyond the given assessment task? I believe we have a problem with generalizability of content because we focus our assessment on the lower level topics. We would find assessment results related to content to be far more reliable in relation to generalizability if we assessed for understanding of the generalizations arising out of the concepts. The generalizations must be supported by specific fact-based examples, which allow us to assess conceptual understanding, specific supporting content, and sophistication in the use of the process skills involved in the task. We assess therefore the three components of the tripartite curriculum model described in Chapter 3 (Figure 3.6).

As an example, if we use the generalization presented earlier related to the concept of "Interdependence"—"Trade is dependent on supply and demand"—secondary school students could be required to do the following:

- Analyze and support the generalization, "Trade is dependent on supply and demand," using specific examples from in-class learning and other current world examples
- Relate the concepts of dependence and interdependence to the concepts of trade and supply and demand

This assessment places the focus on "generalizable" knowledge and skills—the process skill of "analysis" and understanding of a generalization that encompasses many examples across cultures and through time. The generalizability of the content holds to other examples of the stated generalization.

The generalizability of the process of *analysis* is dependent on the conceptual ability (concepts), prior knowledge (critical content), and process skill (applications). We can generalize a student's ability to use a process skill, such as critical thinking, when the performance tasks are matched to the student's developmental level. We can generalize performance to the point that the variables of a task (conceptual, prior knowledge, and process application) are congruent with other tasks.

Designing Performance Assessments for Integrated Teaching Units

Chapter 4 outlined a formula for writing a unit outcome and activity for integrated units of instruction. The unit outcome and activity provide a high-level performance of what the student knows and can do as a result of the unit study. As a significant culmination of the unit study, the outcome and activity carry the most weight in assessment. For this reason, it is important to design a quality *rubric*, or set of criteria, and a standard to direct, define, and assess the quality of work.

Rubrics: General Development

There are four common elements included in a rubric:

1. A set of criteria that outline the expectations for work and serve as the basis for assessment

   - When criteria are set forth for a unit outcome and activity, they need to be articulated clearly with students. For example, assessment criteria for the unit "Media as a Persuasive Force in American Society" might be as follows:

     • Evaluate the forms and applications of media in American society.

     • Analyze the characteristics of persuasion as a force.

     • Design a persuasive advertisement (oral or written) for your new product. Incorporate at least three elements of persuasive advertising.

2. One or more traits that serve as a basis for judging

   - Traits can be identified as the broad categories to be assessed, such as "Content Knowledge" or "Oral Presentation." In the unit "Media as a Persuasive Force in American Society," the expectations for the traits of "Evaluation," "Analysis," and "Design" need to be defined.

3. A definition and indicators to clarify the meaning of each trait

   - The definition and indicators answer the question: "What are the attributes of the trait to be assessed?" For example, how do we define "Oral Presentation?" Attributes might include the following:

     • Clarity: A clear and lucid message

     • Voice: Tone, volume, projection, confidence, feeling tone appropriate

- Stance: Shoulders back, head up, relaxed posture, avoidance of distracting mannerisms and speech habits
- Audience awareness: Monitors and adjusts presentation according to audience reactions

4. A scale of performance with models and indicators for each level
   - *4: Excellent*: The oral presentation is well organized and focused. The presenter makes eye contact with the audience and speaks clearly without distracting mannerisms. The audience is engaged with an appropriate feeling tone. Audience reaction is monitored as the presentation proceeds and appropriate adjustments are made to reengage the audience when necessary.
   - *3: Highly Competent*
   - *2: Competent*
   - *1: Developing*: The oral presentation has a topic focus. Eye contact is made twice with an audience member. Voice tone is audible but variability in feeling tone is yet to be developed. Presentation stance is appropriate.

I have taken the liberty of using the term *developing* at the base level in the above rubric to support the philosophy of developing growth toward a standard and to avoid a deficit model of viewing progress. Students should view assessments as evidence of their "progress" toward the standard. They should also be counseled as to the next stages of development and shown models of the standard work.

Rubric Examples

Figure 5.2 provides a typical rubric model for teachers to use in constructing a task, trait, or generic scoring tool.

Tables 5.1 and 5.2 show examples of rubrics for specific unit outcomes and activities used by teachers in the classrooms. The guiding questions that frame the study are included to illustrate the path of study that leads to the unit outcome and activity.

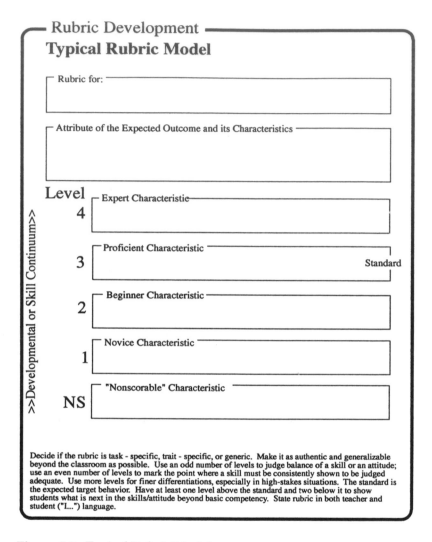

Figure 5.2. Typical Rubric Model
SOURCE: Steve Schuman, Federal Way Public Schools, Federal Way, Washington; used by permission.

Example 1

Concept: *Prejudice*

Unit Theme: *World Prejudice in the Last 50 Years*

Table 5.1 Prejudice Unit Rubric

Excellent	*Highly Competent*	*Competent*
The presentation is characterized by:	The presentation is characterized by:	The presentation is characterized by:
• unusually effective and clear diction	• clear and effective diction	• clear diction
• impeccable grammar	• appropriate grammar	• acceptable grammar
• strict adherence to rules of debate	• adherence to key rules of debate	• adherence to general rules of debate
• well thought out, insightful arguments with strong relevant and specific supporting evidence—historical and contemporary examples along with reasoned historical and contemporary workable solutions • absence of contradictions and fallacies of logic	• well thought out arguments with supporting evidence—adequate historical and contemporary examples along with historical and contemporary workable solutions • absence of contradictions	• arguments with some supporting evidence—a few historical and contemporary examples along with historical and contemporary workable solutions • no major contradictions

SOURCE: Birney Middle School, Charleston, South Carolina; used by permission

Guiding Questions:

- What is prejudice?
- How does one overcome prejudice?
- Can all prejudices be overcome?
- Why does prejudice exist?
- How has prejudice affected your life or the lives of people close to you?

Table 5.2 Rubric for Air Quality Unit

Excellent	*Highly Competent*	*Competent*
The student research is characterized by:	The student research is characterized by:	The student research is characterized by:
• clear, focused writing	• focused writing—somewhat predictable	• generally focused writing
• strong supporting evidence	• basic supporting evidence	• general evidence, but lacking specificity
• thoughtful organization throughout	• logical and consistent organization of topics and paragraphs	• logical organization between topics
• absence of contradiction and fallacies to logic	• absence of contradictions	• no major contradictions
• correct and effective mechanics and usage	• correct mechanics and slight error in usage	• minor usage and mechanical errors do not interfere with comprehension
• precise—accurate and detailed adherence to strand criteria:	• accurate adherence to strand criteria:	• adequate adherence to strand criteria:
–complete consideration of the air quality in South Carolina including industrial, political, economic, and/or social factors	–complete consideration of the air quality in South Carolina including industrial, political, economic, and/or social factors	–consideration of the economic and/or social factors
–thorough treatment of viewpoints presented	–variety of viewpoints presented	–at least two viewpoints presented
–clear, detailed, and plausible . . .	–clear and plausible statement of proposed positions	–adequate statement of proposed positions
–thorough and accurate reporting . . .	–accurate reporting of credible source of information	–generally accurate reporting of credible sources of information

SOURCE: Fort Johnson Middle School, Charleston, South Carolina; used by permission.

- How has prejudice shaped our world today?
- Is prejudice only race related?
- How do students deal with prejudice in the school, and how do you deal with it?
- What is needed in society to reduce and alleviate prejudice?

Unit Outcome and Activity: Evaluate prejudice in the world during the last 50 years to understand the many factors that have caused and continue to cause prejudice. Hold a forum to explore the roots of prejudice and develop possible solutions to overcome prejudice in your lives and in your community.

In the Prejudice Rubric, the student work is not done and will not be accepted until it has reached at least the competent level. The "standard" is set at the highly competent level.

Example 2

Concept: *Pollution*

Unit Theme: *Air Quality in South Carolina*

Guiding Questions:

- What are the health issues involved in air quality?
- What are the sources of air pollution?
- How does legislation govern air quality?
- What is the cost for regulating air quality?
- How do literature and the media address air quality issues?
- How does air quality affect you personally?

Unit Outcome and Activity: Investigate and analyze the air quality in South Carolina to assess the impact on the environment by writing an essay that addresses one or more aspects of air quality on the environment.

Strand Criteria:

- Analyze the air quality in South Carolina including industrial, political, economic, and/or social factors.
- Present current perspectives on the problem from a variety of viewpoints.
- Provide a clear statement of proposed position that forms the basis of your essay.
- Accurately report credible sources of information.
- Show evidence of competence in the writing process.

Portfolios

How do we define a *portfolio?* In a draft paper prepared for an Institute on Assessment Alternatives (1994), Paulson and Paulson provided an adaptation of a definition from the Northwest Evaluation Association:

> A portfolio addresses the question "who am I" and tells a coherent story of the student as learner. It is a purposeful, integrated collection of student work that shows student effort, progress, or achievement in one or more areas. The collection includes evidence of student self-reflection and student participation in setting the focus, establishing the standards, selecting contents, and judging merit. A portfolio tells the student's own story of what is learned and why it is important. (p. 4)

Paulson and Paulson also present an interesting summary of a rubric for judging portfolios that outlines four stages of student growth as shown through the portfolio. This rubric summary is presented in Figure 5.3.

When educators and assessment experts started to look for ways to document and define what students can do, in addition to what they have learned, the portfolio was a natural answer. After all, artists and writers have used portfolios for years to document their work and growing talent.

An *Off-Track* Portfolio

An off-track portfolio is simply a container of student work or assessments without an attempt on the part of the learner to provide organization. There is no attempt by the learner to make a coherent statement about what learning has taken place. The child's understanding of the task is minimal—the portfolio is about "collecting what the teacher asks for." For the student, the portfolio was built by following instructions. Self-reflective statements, if present, add little to clarify organization or explain learning.

An *Emerging* Portfolio

In an emerging portfolio, there is a sense of intentionally controlling some of the student's choices. Students may not be able to verbalize the reasons, even as they reflect on their choices, but the reviewer may be able to recognize a relationship between some exhibits or infer the reasons. Or there may be evidence that the student had some insight into the teacher's purposes. While evidence of self-reflection adds information to the presentation, at this point in the development of the portfolio, there is insufficient information or organization to characterize the portfolio as either a story or learning or a portrait of the learner.

An *On-Track* Portfolio

An on-track portfolio is in the process of becoming a story of the student as an independent learner. There are relationships between one part of the portfolio and another. There is evidence of student ownership. The learner has a personal investment in selecting and explaining the content. It is possible to distinguish other stakeholders' goals from the student's or to recognize instances when they overlap. The portfolio may be created for others to assess, but there is also evidence of self-assessment. The student's voice is always audible.

An *Outstanding* Portfolio

An outstanding portfolio is a coherent story of the student as a reflective learner in which all parts of the portfolio bear a clear relationship to each other and to a central purpose. There is an awareness of the perspectives of other stakeholders, and the student's self-assessment has been enhanced by this knowledge. A reviewer can look at the portfolio and easily understand how the judgments about the learner came to be made and the degree to which different stakeholders would agree. When reviewing the portfolio, outsiders get the feeling they really know the person whose achievement is depicted here and have a fair understanding of how the learning came about.

Figure 5.3. The Four Stages of Portfolio Growth: A Summary of the Rubric for Judging Portfolios

SOURCE: F. Leon Paulson and Pearl Paulson, Multnomah E.S.D., 11611 N.E. Ainsworth Circle, Portland, OR 97220; used by permission.

There were questions that needed to be answered, however.

- How can we measure the contents of a portfolio with valid and reliable results? Are the results generalizable?
- Who selects the items that go into a portfolio?
- Is it possible to develop and measure cross-domain work in a single portfolio? Can the portfolio contain writing samples, mathematics problem solving, art, or even a video presentation?

During the past five years, many questions about the use of portfolios have arisen. Sheila Valencia, in a chapter titled "Portfolios: Panacea or Pandora's Box?" (1991), provides a balanced review of current thinking related to the perceived benefits and concerns related to the use of portfolios. Generally, states Valencia, portfolios have such appeal today because they are *authentic* in terms of the types of activities, setting for the task, alignment with the classroom curriculum, and correlation to current views on learning and cognition.

Other benefits cited in Valencia's (1991) summary include using portfolios to monitor and celebrate a student's skill and knowledge growth over time and to empower teachers, students, and parents. The teacher's professional judgment is valued and is critical to the developmental growth of each child. The child is empowered by engaging in self-reflection and self-evaluation. And, finally, the portfolio empowers the parent because it provides empirical evidence of what his or her child knows and can do. Parents can help guide educational progress and will have a tool to facilitate communication with their child, teachers, and other parents.

On the caution side of the portfolio issue, Valencia (1991) raises questions related to the "purpose, standards, quality, feasibility, and [need for] staff development" (p. 39).

As with most innovations, I see the need for a balanced perspective in regard to the use of portfolios. Three facets of portfolio use that are especially valuable are as follows:

The focus on student self-selection, reflection, and evaluation of portfolio contents: This engenders student responsibility for learning and develops the thinking student.

The focus on assessing each student's developmental growth over time through exhibits of work: This is a positive approach to developmental learning. It is based on value and belief in individual growth rather than on a comparative judgment of worth.

The view of teacher and student as collaborators in the assessment of growth over time. The teacher learns valuable skills for monitoring and assessing developmental learning. This requires critical thinking, analysis, and problem solving. The student and teacher share information and views, and the student feels supported and encouraged.

Though portfolios offer us one of the best tools for authentic assessment, I agree with Valencia and many other leaders in education today that portfolios will not provide all of the answers. They deal more effectively with the process side of development. Until we figure out a better way to show conceptual development related to content, and comparative student data, we will continue to be faced with normative, standardized tests. We must continue to search for a better alternative to address the content side of learning. Perhaps what we learn from portfolios and other forms of performance assessment will lead us to a number 1 alternative for the number 2 bubble sheet dilemma.

Questions and Answers

1. What is a rubric?

Answer: It is a set of criteria and a scale of value to assess work or performance. The rubric specifies the criteria for judging traits and indicators of developmental performance and provides a standard of excellence.

2. What is a standard?

Answer: It is a set point for quality (not minimal) performance against which student growth can be measured developmentally and over time.

3. How should teachers view standards?

Answer: Teachers should view a standard as a goal for each student. This means developing and implementing support strategies to help each child move along the continuum of progress. It also means refusing to accept work that has shown no effort. It means expecting the best effort and providing support to ensure success.

4. How do we grade learning disability or slower achieving students?

Answer: I would rather we *assess* than *grade*. The assessment should be based on how much growth the student has made over time, toward the standard, if we are measuring developmental process skills such as writing or speaking. Conveying this growth to the child and parent through the use of work samples, scales of growth, or developmental indicators is preferable to a letter grade. If required to give letter grades, then the grade should be based on the evident growth, but there also needs to be a narrative description, or method, for showing the developmental level (e.g., Beginning, Intermediate, Advanced).

5. How do we grade mastery of content?

Answer: Because content is not a personal, developmental process, you can grade the student's mastery differently. Letter grades are more appropriate for evaluating mastery of content. How much content a student has learned is a quantitative matter, but if you are assessing the student's personal thinking ability in relation to the understanding of content, then you are back into a developmental growth assessment. In any case, however, letter grades are a weak form for conveying depth of knowledge and ability to perform.

6. Why is there so much emphasis today on the design of performance rubrics?

Answer: There is increasing emphasis on rubrics because they help clarify our teaching outcomes for students. Teachers often find, as they design the rubrics, that their assessment activity does not really address the critical outcomes they wish to measure. High-quality rubrics clarify the assessment criteria and standards for process performance and content knowledge. Teachers often adjust their assessment activity after developing the rubric. They strive to align the task with the expected outcomes as defined by rubric criteria and standards.

SUMMARY

In the frenzy to meet the economic, social, and political demands of an interdependent world, government and business have teamed to set an agenda for schools. National and state governmental bodies legislate academic standards, and subject area committees work to define what students must know and be able to do by high school graduation.

This movement can be helpful to schools if the issues of time and funding for training and technology are addressed. If the assessments that accompany the national and state standards involve high stakes, and issues such as training and inequitable resources and opportunity have not been addressed, the plans will fail. States that address the classroom issues related to the attainment of standards will have the greatest chance of success.

Demands for higher levels of performance in what students know and can do are causing a tidal wave in the testing community. Old paradigms of bell-shaped curves; normative, standardized testing; reliability, validity, and generalizability are all shaken up.

New forms, called alternative assessments, are claiming their "authentic" role in meeting the new educational demands. Teachers attend workshops and conferences, feeling the pressure to understand the talk of portfolios and performance assessments. But the assessment experts are only one step ahead, and the answers to questions are still being debated. Slowly, however, the mist is beginning to lift and a common language and belief system are emerging.

Performance assessments are carried out in classrooms. They measure what students know and can do through complex tasks that combine content and process skills. A rubric sets the criteria and standard for the performance. What used to be a letter grade with a few subjective comments now appears as a numerical and/or qualitative scale of performance descriptors, or indicators.

Portfolios tell a story of the student's growth in knowledge and skill over time. The student self-evaluates his or her work according to defined criteria and a standard. The goals are student responsibility and increased learning.

New forms of assessment squeeze in beside the old. At times they bump against each other. The fit is not comfortable. Teachers prefer the newer forms, and the public prefers the old. But the two must share space until educators develop the newer forms to a level that satisfies public questions and concerns.

Extending Thought

1. How do traditional report cards need to change to reflect process development as well as content knowledge?

2. If you were the public relations director for your school, how would you help parents see the value of performance assessment? How would you address their concerns with standardized test scores?

3. What is a "performance assessment?"

4. How can performance assessment assist you in meeting the educational needs of your students?

5. How does "self-assessment" contribute to the development of independent learners?

6. What is the teacher's responsibility in teaching to a standard for each child? What happens in schools when the standard is only assumed to be for the top 30% of the student population?

CHAPTER 6

Stirring the
Head, Heart, and Soul

Creating a Love of Learning

The classroom buzzes with activity. Children work in small groups intent on discovering the mysteries of life: How do birds fly? Just what is in those owl pellets? How do caterpillars change into butterflies? Why don't animals talk like humans? What would happen if the desert suddenly gained rivers? The teacher circulates from group to group—listening, asking probing questions, suggesting resources, and encouraging the efforts. Students express ideas; their friends question and extend the thinking. New ideas emerge.

The room is rich with material. Student work lines the walls, and books, art prints, science materials, and mathematics manipulatives are evident in the plentiful work space. Students use desktop computers and build reports on their findings. They access databases to find material relevant to the theme under study and compare notes on global pollution with students around the world. They use "digital chisel" or build "hypercard stacks" to display their knowledge and scan in pictures to enhance the graphic appeal. Buttons on the hypercard stacks call in portions of a laser videodisc related to the topic. These are the students of the computer age.

Down the hall, in another classroom, students sit in rows and stare at their social studies textbook while child after child reads a paragraph or two. The teacher perches on a stool in the front of the room and asks questions about the facts just read. Some posters hang on the wall, and books sit in tidy position on the shelves, sorted by size. The room is quiet except for the bored drone of the student reading and a bee that works furiously to escape through a window.

Stirring the Head

Brain-Based Learning

Teachers are the architects for learning. They design the environments for developing minds. Caine and Caine (1991), in an important book called *Teaching and the Human Brain,* differentiate between "surface knowledge" and "meaningful knowledge." Surface knowledge is referred to as the traditional memorization of facts and procedures. To be meaningful, however, students must be able to perceive relationships and patterns to make sense of information. Students make sense of information by relating it to their unique past experience and the current environmental context and interactions (Caine & Caine, 1991). New experiences bring expanded conceptions as learners interact and discover knowledge.

Brain research supports the thesis that meaningful education is based on complex and concrete activities that engage students' minds, hearts, and emotions. Caine and Caine (1991) state that "brain-based learning" involves the following:

- Designing and orchestrating lifelike, enriching, and appropriate experiences for learners
- Ensuring that students process experience in such a way as to increase the extraction of meaning

Brain-based learning supports the current movement to integrate curriculum as an effective way to facilitate the brain's search for patterns and connections. An integrated curriculum also develops depth of understanding by presenting a message through a variety of contexts and disciplines (Caine & Caine, 1991).

A key point in the Caine and Caine (1991) text involves the ideas of "disequilibrium" and "self-reorganization." Disequilibrium occurs "when the original state of equilibrium is disturbed" (p. 19). When a learner meets new information that is confusing or disturbing, he or she enters a mental state of disequilibrium. This state is reconciled when "the learner moves to a broader or more inclusive notion—a more sophisticated schema or [mental] map (Cowan, 1978; Doll, 1986)" (Caine & Caine, 1991, p. 129).

Caine and Caine also quote Doll (1989) on the use of the concept of disequilibrium through an experiment in teaching mathematics:

> The concept of self-organization through disequilibrium meant we had to organize the Friday curriculum and our presentation of it in such a manner that we had enough of a "burr" to stimulate the students into rethinking their habitual methods but not so much of a burr that reorganization would fall apart or not be attempted. Maintaining this dynamic tension between challenge and comfort was one of the skills we had to perfect. (pp. 67-68)

As architects for learning, teachers realize that a classroom built on traditional, control-oriented structures is antithetical to the engagement of reasoning, creative minds. As teachers move from old models of instruction, they develop new ways of viewing.

- Teachers need *some* wisdom, not *all* wisdom.

  - In the newer models of instruction, teachers have enough wisdom to know key lessons to be learned from content instruction, but they look forward to learning more lessons along with their students as they construct and share new knowledge.

- The textbook is only one tool for gaining information.

  - The learning environment is resource rich, with computers, magazines, videos, books, and dialogue corners for exploring ideas among friends. The community is an extension of the classroom and students give service to learn social responsibility and the application of knowledge to life.

- *Tight control* is replaced by *purposeful enthusiasm.*

  - The teacher recognizes that a purposeful, enthusiastic search for knowledge engages the student's self-direction; the teacher becomes a structural design engineer and "facilitator" rather than a maintenance engineer and "controller."

Thinking Teachers for Thinking Students

It is common talk today that students who take responsibility for their learning are more interested and engaged with the subject at hand. The same holds true for teachers. Teachers who take responsibility for the design, delivery, and assessment of curriculum and instruction show greater interest and engagement with the learning process. Districts that encourage teachers to design quality curricula to use in their classrooms stimulate higher levels of thoughtfulness in teaching.

Teachers who depend on textbooks or on the nebulous "they" to tell them what and how to teach are not thinking. Thinking teachers work within the required curricular structure, but they personalize the design for student learning by thinking deeply and creatively about students, outcomes, and their plans for curriculum and instruction.

Teachers hold a clear vision of student success and challenge themselves to draw out the best efforts. They think on their feet and watch for opportunities to pop provocative questions. The "right" answer isn't always as important as the thoughtful rationale.

Student Engagement and Constructivist Views

Though the constructivist terminology is popular today, the philosophical basis for the ideas have been around since the days of educators and philosophers such as Pestalozzi, Froebel, Herbart,

Dewey, and James. As with most trends in education, the term *constructivist* has a continuum of interpretations.

Jacqueline Grennon Brooks and Martin Brooks, in a booklet titled *The Case for Constructivist Classrooms* (1993), provide a set of teaching behaviors that they believe can be used to frame the constructivist methodology. The first behavior is at the heart of a purist, constructivist philosophy, so I have provided a short extension of the thought. This is followed by the remaining teaching behaviors identified by the authors.

Constructivist teachers encourage and accept student autonomy. Students take responsibility for learning by posing questions and issues and searching for answers, connections, and possible new problems. The teacher's frame for an assignment affects the degree of autonomy and student initiative for learning. Heavy lecture and overcontrol of student work robs students of opportunities to be self-reliant thinkers. According to Brooks and Brooks (1993, pp. 103-118), constructivist teachers

- use raw data and primary sources, along with manipulative, interactive, and physical materials;
- use cognitive terminology such as "classify," "analyze," "predict," and "create" when framing tasks;
- allow student responses to drive lessons, shift instructional strategies, and alter content;
- inquire about students' understandings of concepts before sharing their own understanding of those concepts;
- encourage students to engage in dialogue, both with the teacher and with one another;
- encourage student inquiry by asking thoughtful, open-ended questions and encouraging students to ask questions of each other;
- seek elaboration of students' initial responses;
- engage students in experiences that might engender contradictions to their initial hypotheses and then encourage discussion;
- allow wait time after posing questions;

- provide time for students to construct relationships and create metaphors;
- nurture students' natural curiosity through frequent use of the learning cycle model. (Brooks & Brooks, 1993, pp. 103-118)

The authors end the discussion on teaching descriptors with the statement: "These descriptors can serve as guides that may help other educators forge personal interpretations of what it means to become a constructivist teacher" (p. 118).

My personal interpretation of the constructivist ideas supports all of the teaching behaviors outlined in the Brooks's listing but deviates from a purist belief system on one significant point. I believe it is possible to have students initiate the search for knowledge, discover connections, and construct personal conceptual frameworks within the context of an articulated core content curriculum. The key, as the Brooks's booklet stated, is how the teacher frames the assignments. Is the area under study framed by open-ended "guiding questions" that engage the student's interest and intellect?

Students do not always need to decide on the problems for study, though they should have opportunities to do so. The currently popular "Project Approach" is an example of the purist constructivist philosophy in action. Students decide on, or are given by the teacher, a problem, issue, concept, or topic to pursue. The questions for study are open ended and engage students in the search for and construction of knowledge. My problem with using this open project-as-you-go approach is that it fails to address the need for a developmental core content curriculum. The articulation of a core content curriculum and expected learnings appears antithetical, in the purist perspective, to the processes of constructing and creating knowledge.

I believe, however, that students need to balance the acquisition of conceptually based content learnings and the development of lifelong processing skills. Teachers need to know some of the key generalizations that students will discover as they work with units of study. If teachers do not have these key learnings in mind as they facilitate the students' search for knowledge, how can they know which questions to ask to stimulate deeper thought?

Suppose that Mr. Jackson has engaged his high school students in a unit based on the concept "Persuasion." The theme of the unit is "Media as a Persuasive Force in American Society." Students have brainstormed many questions to guide their search for knowledge: Is the media a positive or negative force in society? How do the media affect public opinion? How are the media controlled? What is the role of the media in a society?

Mr. Jackson begins the unit by finding out the student conceptions of "persuasion." As they begin searching for answers and debating positions, Mr. Jackson uses effective questions to challenge the students to mentally rise above the many examples of media persuasion. He wants them to discover the deeper ideas, or generalizations, related to the concept of persuasion. If he has not taken his own thinking to this level, then students will end their learning with simplistic answers.

To illustrate with an example, a simple response to the question, "How do the media affect public opinion?" might be "by using propaganda techniques to sway thinking." But the teacher who wants students to discover the deeper lessons of persuasion would question further, "How does propaganda sway thinking?" Dialogue and discussion on this question could lead to the higher level generalization, "Propaganda appeals to beliefs, values, and emotions." The teacher continues to question, "How?" "Why?" "When?" "Is this good or bad?"

When students are given opportunities to deal with life-relevant questions, problems, and issues, they feel a need to know. They develop analytical and critical thinking skills as they research, probe, dialogue, and defend positions. A particularly effective strategy asks students to take one position on an issue and then defend the polar position to gain insight into varying perspectives.

One of the problems with traditional content curriculum is that it usually fails to make the significant connections to events and trends of the day. The textbook study is dry, dull, and lacks relevance for the student. The challenge for teachers is to help bring meaning to the students' learning.

One key to meaningfulness is to teach to the lessons that transfer through time, using events and content as examples, rather than end products, of the learnings. Another key is to help students find the connections between past and present events. A third suggestion is to apply the teaching behaviors of a constructivist philosophy. Students who are motivated to take responsibility in the search for knowledge will see greater relevance in the content under study.

If there were one single factor that would revolutionize education and bring success for all children, I believe it would be the constructivist notion that students who are motivated to take responsibility for their own learning will be successful learners. But to bring about this situation, we would need to change many traditions in education:

- Teachers would need to forget the bell-shaped curve and believe that all children can, and should, be successful learners.
- The deficit model of letter grading developmental processes would have to go. The new paradigm would celebrate success as students move along a continuum in reading, writing, thinking, communicating, drawing, dramatizing, or any other developing process.
- The pursuit of trivia would be replaced by curricula that hold meaningfulness or importance for students. By what criteria should we define *critical content* for the 21st century?
- Teachers would need to continue the development of personal capacities in critical and creative thinking to challenge and motivate their students to even higher levels of knowing and performing.
- Curriculum and assessment would have to move from bits of study to coherent, in-depth, and integrated units of study. The big ideas would be the focus for content instruction.
- Teachers would know when to lead, and when to follow, in supporting each child's journey to self-responsibility.
- The current trend to have students (and teachers) self-reflect on their work according to defined criteria and standards would need to continue.

Excellence in the Basic Skills for All

I am going to say it: *The most important job of kindergarten, first-grade, and second-grade teachers is to ensure that every child can read, write, listen, speak, think, create, and compute.* If the learning environment for these process skills is positive and supportive and the home life is stable, then the student will be successful. Success will engender a healthy esteem. It does little good to spend half a day on self-esteem activities if the child feels like a failure every time he or she looks at a book. The time is better spent on building literacy and fostering individual creative expression. Self-esteem is nurtured at school through the ongoing positive interactions between the child and the teacher and between the child and classmates. Self-esteem building is not a 15-minute program four times a week.

Children who are not academically successful in the primary grades usually fall further and further behind as they proceed through school. With a 30% drag at the primary level, it is no surprise that we have a 30% dropout rate in high school.

Primary grade teachers, like their colleagues at the other levels, have been affected by increasing curricular and societal demands. They feel (and sometimes are) compelled to teach every topic and every special program, from tarantulas to teeth. But the reality is that these teachers will not be able to meet the needs of all of their developing learners if they aren't freed from the overdemands on their classroom time. Add to the heavy curriculum the interruptions caused by intercom announcements and assemblies (a schoolwide problem), and we have a serious time problem.

Students apply literacy skills in the context of content-based curricula. Teachers at the primary level should be allowed to teach to broad-based units of study in social studies and science and then apply the process skills within the integrated units. Art, music, and literature can fit into these units according to the concept and theme under study. Health can fit into integrated science theme units. Mathematics has application across all fields of study. By teaching to broad units of study, teachers will have more time to meet the needs of individual students and ensure their success.

At the primary level, the teachers must "teach" students the process skills of reading, writing, and so on. *Teach* means direct instruction, and opportunities for application, with the critical skills necessary for successful performance. Critical skills in reading aren't the hundreds of microskills that used to fill up the front of teachers' manuals, but they are the essential components for being able to decode words, read fluently, gain meaning, and construct knowledge. This instruction is time consuming and challenging because of the beginning development of our littlest learners. Most of these abilities can be gained effectively in the literature-rich environment espoused by Whole Language advocates. The best approach for developing decoding abilities, however, is still a controversial matter.

In my travels around the country during the past year, I have noticed a distinct swing back toward systematic phonics instruction in beginning reading. Teachers say that students are not able to decode fluently using the purist Whole Language approach of teaching sounds as needed, and in an embedded word context. This revelation did not surprise me—but I was surprised that so many teachers in our country so readily bought into whole class reading and drastically deemphasized phonics methods.

Stirring the Heart and Soul

Joanna was in the 11th grade. Her grandparents were survivors of the Holocaust. She wanted to share their story with her classmates as her English project but knew that a simple retelling would not convey the depth of pain, degradation, and grief that spun their world in the concentration camps. Joanna spent hours talking with her grandparents, internalizing their thoughts, fears, anger, and hopes as they recounted the terrible years.

Joanna searched for the Holocaust videos that showed families being herded onto trains traveling to annihilation. She pieced film clips together to build a montage of images—fearful children clinging to mothers; husbands, wives, and babies crying as they were separated; faces of questioning—then pain: smoke paving a trail toward the heavens; sunken eyes and gaunt bodies hanging onto fences like skeletons left behind.

On the day of the class presentation, Joanna portrayed her grandmother as a young teenage girl, reliving the Holocaust as she had experienced it. As the video silently rolled through the stirring scenes, Joanna sat beside the monitor and poured out the personal story of loss and grief, of pain and fear, of hatred and hope.

The students sat quietly, riveted to the emotional performance. Questions hung in the air waiting to be discussed: "How could humans treat other humans in this way?" "How do people find the strength to survive when their families are destroyed?" "Could this happen again?"

Joanna stirred her classmates. They felt personally involved in the human story. As a finale to the presentation, Joanna introduced her grandparents to the class. They shared how they had moved on to rebuild their lives and ended with a plea, "Never forget the lessons of the Holocaust. Be always on the lookout for one person's inhumanity to another, whether it be on your street or in a far corner of the world."

Joanna's presentation stimulated a general discussion of contemporary examples of people's inhumanity to one another. Students looked to the deeper reasons underlying the acts of inhumanity, such as fear, ignorance, and prejudice. They talked of the ramifications of inhumane acts and considered the question, "How 'civilized' is humankind?"

Feeling Teachers for Feeling Students

Joanna's teacher encouraged his students to express their passion for the subject matter in their presentations. He modeled enthusiasm for thoughts, ideas, and knowledge. Whether the subject under discussion engendered empathy, anger, joy, or pride, the teacher demonstrated the role of emotion. Joanna could have told the students her grandparents' story as if she were reading an essay, but the students would not have experienced their pain. They soon would have forgotten the lessons. When feelings are tapped in a nonthreatening environment, learning can be enhanced.

Teachers are caring individuals who reach out to each child, intent on fostering academic, social, and emotional development. They recognize that the child's personality is a fragile work in progress.

They manage their own emotional lives privately and focus in school on supporting each child in myriad ways:

- Modeling values and ethics—positive enthusiasm, empathy, reason, dialogue in conflict, honesty, and caring
- Knowing and connecting interpersonally with each child—asking each one about his or her thoughts, activities, and opinions
- Supporting risk taking—encouraging each child to try, even if he or she fails, and setting an environment of trust and belief in abilities
- Building on success—valuing quality effort and praising growth
- Providing clear directions and expectations—setting the stage for quality learning
- Allowing and planning for different patterns of learning—getting out the magnifying glass to read the work of the gifted writer who discovered that by writing microscopically one could get more thoughts on a page
- Seeing the giftedness in the perceived problem children—the "verbal motor mouth," the "graffiti artist," the "takeover leader," and the "social butterfly"

When teachers delight in the uniqueness of children, they come to know each child well. They take the time to find out a child's likes and dislikes, their interests and questions. They look for the gift that each child brings and take opportunities to fan the ember into flame. They see in the shy boy a desire to lead and in the crude drawing of a little girl an unusual expression of deep emotion. They mention their observations and provide opportunities, guidance, and encouragement as the children realize they have gifts to develop.

In secondary schools—where students shuffle from class to class in 50-minute intervals, and bells fragment subjects, discussions, thinking, and learning—teachers have little time to discover the unique gifts of students. With up to 150 students per day flowing in and out, the first day's greeting, "I want to get to know you," becomes a major task.

Some secondary schools have restructured the use of time, personnel, and curriculum to solve the problems of too much to teach, too little time, and too many lost teenagers. Schools-within-a-school divide the student population and assign them to a multidisciplinary team of teachers. They plan a curriculum that can be offered in longer blocks of time so that students do not have to change classes every hour. Each teacher takes responsibility for personally connecting with an assigned group of students so that they have someone to turn to with questions or for help.

As teachers have more time with students in class, they are more aware of students who need help and draw on resources to assist. The school has open communication channels with community agencies and calls for their help when necessary. Parents are contacted when a child is having trouble in school, and joint efforts prevent growing despair.

In some schools, the same group of teachers keep their assigned students for more than one year. This allows a greater bond of understanding and respect to develop between students and teachers. When they enter school in the fall, students pick up where they left off and time is not lost while new teachers assess what the students know.

Many elementary schools are also keeping a group of students with one teacher for multiple years. This provides greater security for the child and allows the teacher to know each child personally. Elementary teachers have always believed in nurturing the development of each child, but some feel that even a full year with a child does not provide enough time to find and foster his or her unique talents and abilities. These teachers also desire the extended years with a child to provide a smooth transition and ongoing development of their educational program.

Finally, keeping a group of students for multiple years allows students to know their teacher as a social human being with dreams, interests, and talents. In a classroom that stirs the head, heart, and soul, the teacher interacts positively with students. This teacher is passionate about learning and conveys the excitement to students.

Stimulating the Creative Spirit

When we talk of a passion for learning that stirs the heart and soul, we talk of a creative spirit. Minds that are eager to create deliver with enthusiasm. Just as we provide students with opportunities to dialogue to gain insight into the meaning of content, so must we provide opportunities for students to create and evaluate through various forms of artistic expression.

Eliott Eisner, in *The Educational Imagination* (1994), discusses the idea of connoisseurship in the arts as "knowledgeable perception" and appreciation. Eisner (1994) emphasizes that perception and appreciation for a work of art require a "sensory memory" (p. 215). The connoisseur must draw from memory the sensory comparisons made over a range of experiences in a particular mode of expression. Connoisseurship, says Eisner (1994), goes beyond mere recognition of artistic aspects to the perception of subtleties, complexities, and important aspects of a work.

The traditional educational emphases on linguistic and mathematical forms of representation and the generally weak teacher training in arts education have shortchanged our students. How can we engender the developing qualities of a connoisseur in our children? How can we help them appreciate the subtle stories in their own work? How can we help them use the arts as a form of unique personal expression and as a way of viewing, representing, and thinking?

In *Frames of Mind* (1993), Howard Gardner provides a valuable service to children in calling for educational valuing of multiple forms of intelligence. Spatial intelligence, expressed in part through the arts, is one form of intelligence described by Gardner. But simply providing more standardized "art activities"—colored cutout bunnies with cotton ball tails or copy paper snowflakes to frame the bulletin board—will not develop the arts intelligence to the level of subtle nuance and expression.

When students use the skills of connoisseurship to assess the work in their creative products, whether a piece of pottery, a dance, a visual display, or a musical presentation, they expand their intelligence by integrating technical, sensory, emotional, and interpretive ways of knowing. This unique and complex response values and supports the developing mind.

Students who learn how to express their unique thoughts and ideas through multiple modalities have broadened opportunities for taking personal responsibility in learning. They are not dependent on the linguistic road to independence.

Loving to Learn

The Passionate Learner

Passion—boundless enthusiasm, zeal, interest, excitement—is the antithesis of boredom. The passionate learner is every teacher's dream. But in a room of 30, we are likely to find a handful of these enthusiasts. What does the passionate learner look like? How can we help all children find interest and excitement in learning?

The passionate learner shares his or her interest and enthusiasm in a variety of ways. You see a beaming face and glistening eyes as the student proudly holds up his or her work to be admired. You notice intense concentration as a problem is solved or a piece of work is crafted to quality. Excited talk fills the room as thoughts and ideas are shared between team members making new discoveries. Or you see an introspective child, off in a corner, engrossed in a book on rocks and minerals—a future geologist.

What do these students have in common that qualifies them as passionate learners?

- *a love of learning*—a realization that information brings interesting ideas, that new information can be connected to prior information to solve problems and make discoveries
- *inquisitive minds*—questioning attitudes that seek to know answers
- *self-value*—students who care about themselves and value their personal thoughts and ideas

How easy our job would be if all students maintained these qualities throughout their school years. But the reality is that too many students fail to hold these attributes, for a host of reasons. Perhaps their response to a threatening environment, at home or in school, is to shut down and withdraw. Or perhaps they have not yet realized that thought is a tool for self-discovery and definition.

Teaching is an art of individual prescription. Even though we may at times teach the group, we must know every child and their

Passion for Learning Index Chart	
Nurtures	**Hinders**
+60 Teacher as facilitator of learning	−50 Occasional sarcasm to disruptive students
+50 Support for risk taking	−80 Deficit model for assessing process development, as in writing
+70 Open dialogue; thinking focus	−30 Too open—unclear structure for the constructivist philosophy
+80 Cooperative learning	−20 Letter-grade and time-driven evaluations
+90 Valuing of all students; interpersonal connecting	−60 Performances usually written or spoken rather than allowing other modalities such as art, drama, or music
+350 Total	−240 Total

Figure 6.1. Nurturing the Passionate Learner

educational needs as individuals. We cannot assume that every child will naturally be a passionate learner, with an inquisitive mind and a healthy self-ethos.

We spend so much time in school focusing on the content we teach. A few students voraciously absorb the information. They have the attributes of the passionate learner. Some students dutifully memorize the required content and enter class with their pencils poised, ready to "go for the silver or bronze." And about a third of the class sit back in their chairs with a glazed look in their eyes, trying to figure out the easiest way to pass the test with the least amount of effort. Finally, we have the bottom two seat-warmers, who find school so excruciatingly painful that they count the days to their 16th birthdays.

Could we reach more of our children if we assessed the learning environment for its ability to nurture passionate learners? Are there things going on in classrooms that destroy the passion that young children bring to school? I will share some ideas in this regard, but I encourage every teacher to evaluate their own classroom and come up with a "Passion for Learning Index." First, list all of the attributes of the learning environment in your classroom that *nurture* the passionate learner. Then, in a second column, list all of the attributes that *hinder* the passionate learner.

For each item in the nurture column, assign plus points from 1 to 100, according to impact. Assign minus points to items in the hinder column. The points are your subjective judgment as to the negative or positive impact value of each item. The higher the point value, the greater the positive or negative impact. Total points should not exceed 350 in either column. Figure 6.1 provides a sample listing to stimulate thought.

Once the points are assigned to the nurture/hinder items, the "Passion for Learning Index" can be determined by subtracting the negative points from the positive. In the example provided in Figure 6.1, the index is +110. This result is your assessment of how well you nurture the critical qualities found in passionate learners. The higher your score—the closer you come to 350—the more enthusiasm you should see for learning. The teacher in Figure 6.1 needs to address some critical aspects to raise the score. This passionate learner index can also be determined for your school as a whole by doing the exercise as a total staff.

Now comes the important step. What are you going to do about your negative scores? Develop your action plan, implement your strategies for change, and monitor the results by watching those passionate learners come to life!

A Challenge to Teachers and Parents

Most children are naturally inquisitive. You can see it in their eyes at one year of age. They study their environment, and you notice thoughtfulness as they see a live kitten for the first time. Their interest is sparked and they toddle on chubby little legs after the vanishing ball of fur—eager to grab the strange little creature and examine it more closely.

The responsibility to nurture curiosity is a challenging task. It means being patient with the pesky questions that always seem too complicated to answer: "Where do babies come from?" "Why are leaves green?" Or, from a Los Angeles classroom, "Why can't we 'just all get along?'"

It means expanding the experience base of the child—reading books together, traveling, hiking the nature trails, talking, sharing, laughing, playing—using all of the senses to interact with the environment and to construct conceptual perspectives.

It means positively affirming children's ideas and efforts as they explore new territory. It means realizing that children are composed of many parts—minds, hearts, emotions, and bodies—all developing toward an integrated whole. It means continually stirring the head, heart, and soul and loving all children so that they love themselves.

SUMMARY

Teachers and parents are partners. They share the job of nurturing the head, heart, and soul of a child. In their own ways, they contribute to the development of self-esteem, confidence, and the important belief in self. They look for the child's strengths and gifts and build on each successful try. They ensure competence in the basic skills of schooling and provide experiences that continually expand what the child knows and can do.

Teachers design the environment for learning. Control-oriented structures are being replaced by busy, purposeful settings where students take increasing responsibility for constructing knowledge.

New skills beckon teachers to workshops and conferences. They realize that preparing students for the future is as complex as the future itself. Teachers of today must use higher level thinking, processing vast amounts of information related to the students they teach, the abstract and essential learnings of content, and the most effective instructional strategies for each situation. A teacher's organized mind brings clarity to complexity and focus to an educational vision.

Children who love to learn do so with their heads, hearts, and souls. Teachers who have a passion for teaching and learning and a keen interest in the development of each child engage students in wanting to know—to explore questions and issues that extend from their world.

Loving to learn is a gift. In some, it is a natural quest of an inquisitive mind. In others, it is an undiscovered well, covered over with untapped talent. Creating a love of learning means discovering a wellspring of talent, supporting the flow of energy, and celebrating success along the way.

I invite you to share the gift and the secret of loving to learn—stirring the head, heart, and soul.

Glossary

Benchmarks: Agreed-upon developmental mileposts.

Block scheduling: Extended class periods at the secondary school level; intended to allow for curricular coordination or integration of compatible subject areas.

Career paths: Theme-based organizational structure for high schools that facilitates a school-to-work transition plan.

Concept: A mental construct that frames a set of examples sharing common attributes; high-level concepts are timeless, universal, abstract, and broad. Examples: Cycles, Diversity, Interdependence.

Constructivist: A philosophy and methodology for teaching and learning that highlights the student construction of knowledge on a path to learner autonomy.

Cooperative learning: A teaching strategy that groups students in pairs or teams to problem solve, discover, and discuss ideas or investigate topics of interest.

Curriculum: The planned curriculum is an educational response to the needs of society and the individual and requires that the learner construct knowledge, attitudes, values, and skills through a complex interplay of mind, materials, and social interactions.

Curriculum framework: A planning guide for educators that states subject area content and process outcomes in general terms.

Developmentally appropriate: Refers to the match between the learning task and the student's cognitive, social, or physical ability to perform the task successfully.

Generalizations: Two or more concepts stated as a relationship— essential learnings; the "big ideas" related to the critical concepts and topics of a subject. Example: Freedom is the basis of democracy.

Indicators: Observable behaviors that reflect a point on a skill or knowledge continuum.

Integrated curriculum: The organization of interdisciplinary content under a common, abstract concept such as "Interdependence" or "Conflict."

Interdisciplinary: A variety of disciplines sharing a common, conceptual focus for study.

Multidisciplinary: A variety of disciplines coordinated to a topic of study; lacking a conceptual focus.

Objectives: Specific statements of what you want students to know; specific content or skill focus; measurable, usually by paper-and-pencil test.

Outcomes: Broad statements of what you want students to know and be able to do as a result of teaching/learning.

Performance assessment: A complex demonstration of content knowledge and performance assessed according to a standard and a set of criteria; shows what students know and can do.

Portfolio: A chosen collection of student work and self-assessment that is used to showcase excellence or to demonstrate progress on a developmental performance.

Process skills: Internal student abilities that develop in sophistication over time. Examples: reading, writing, speaking, thinking, drawing, singing, dramatizing, and so on.

Rubric: A multilevel set of criteria to show/measure development in assessing work or performance toward an instructional outcome.

Standard: An agreed-upon definition of quality performance.

Systems thinking: A framework for looking at interrelationships and patterns of change over time (Senge, 1990); critical for successful school restructuring.

Topical theme: A content topic that grounds the study of conceptually based, integrated units; provides focus and meaningfulness to the student's work; may or may not restate the concept. Example: "The Rise and Fall of Prejudice in American Society."

Tripartite curriculum model: A balanced approach to concepts, critical content, and developmental process in teaching and assessment.

Whole Language: A popular belief system in teaching that integrates the language arts and stresses quality literature and immersion in reading and writing, and shares the constructivist views. Students build on prior knowledge and take personal responsibility for self-assessment of progress.

References

Arizona Department of Education. (1992). *The Arizona model for vocational/technological education.* Phoenix: Author.

Baker, E. L. (1994, January). *The use of performance assessments.* Keynote presentation at the Fourth Annual International Conference on Restructuring Curriculum-Assessment-Teaching for the 21st Century, National School Conference Institute, Phoenix, AZ.

Banks, J. A. (1991). *Teaching strategies for ethnic studies.* Boston: Allyn & Bacon.

Banks, J. A. (1992, May 15-17). *Multicultural education and school reform.* Revised version of presentation at the American Forum Conference, Philadelphia, PA.

Brooks, J. G., & Brooks, M. G. (1993). *The case for constructivist classrooms.* Alexandria, VA: Association for Supervision and Curriculum Development.

Caine, R. N., & Caine, G. (1991). *Teaching and the human brain.* Alexandria, VA: Association for Supervision and Curriculum Development.

Copa, G. H., & Pease, V. H. (1992). *New designs for the comprehensive high school* (Vol. 2). Berkeley: University of California, National Center for Research in Vocational Education.

Council of Chief State School Officers with the National Council for Geographic Education. (1994). *The national geography assessment framework.* Washington, DC: Author.

Cowan, P. A. (1978). *Piaget with feeling: Cognitive, social and emotional dimensions.* New York: Holt, Rinehart & Winston.

Daggett, W. (1991, June). *The changing nature of work: A challenge to education.* Keynote address at the joint summer conference, Association of Washington School Principals and Washington Association of School Administrators.

David Douglas High School. (1992). *Project Stars.* Portland, OR: Portland School District.

Doll, W. E. J. (1986). *Curriculum beyond stability: Schon, Prigogine, Piaget.* Unpublished manuscript.

Doll, W. E. J. (1989). Complexity in the classroom. *Educational Leadership, 47*(1), 65-70.

Eisner, E. W. (1994). *The educational imagination.* New York: Macmillan.

Florida Department of Education. (1989). *Blueprint for career preparation.* Tallahassee: Author.

Gardner, H. (1993). *Frames of mind: The theory of multiple intelligences.* New York: Basic Books.

Harste, J. C., & Burke, C. L. (1993, March 20). *Planning to plan: Supporting inquiry in classrooms.* Paper presented at the Curriculum Planning Workshop on Whole Language, Tacoma, WA.

Jacobs, H. H. (1989). *Interdisciplinary curriculum: Design and implementation.* Alexandria, VA: Association for Supervision and Curriculum Development.

Johnston, W. B. (1991, March-April). Global work force 2000: The new world labor market. *Harvard Business Review,* pp. 115-127.

Kleibard, H. M. (1993). What is a knowledge base, and who would use it if we had one? *Review of Educational Research, 63*(3), 295-303.

Marzano, R. J. (1992). *A different kind of classroom: Teaching with dimensions of learning.* Aurora, CO: Mid-continent Regional Educational Laboratory.

Marzano, R. J., Pickering, D., & McTighe, J. (1993). *Assessing student outcomes: Performance assessment using the dimensions of learning model.* Aurora, CO: Mid-continent Regional Educational Laboratory.

National Council for the Social Studies (NCSS). (1992). *Definition of social studies* (single-page statement). Washington, DC: Author.

National Council of Social Studies (NCSS). (1994). *National standards for social studies.* Washington, DC: Author.

National Council of Teachers of Mathematics. (1991). *Professional standards for teaching mathematics* (Executive summary). Reston, VA: Author.

Paul, R. W. (1993a). A model for the assessment of higher order thinking. In J. Willsen & A. J. A. Binker (Eds.), *Critical thinking: How to prepare students for a rapidly changing world* (pp. 103-151). Santa Rosa, CA: Foundation for Critical Thinking.

Paul, R. W. (1993b). Using intellectual standards to assess student reasoning. In J. Willsen & A. J. A. Binker (Eds.), *Critical thinking: How to prepare students for a rapidly changing world* (pp. 153-164). Santa Rosa, CA: Foundation for Critical Thinking.

Paulson, F. L., & Paulson, P. R. (1994). *A guide for judging portfolios.* Portland, OR: Multnomah Educational Service District.

Popham, J. (1993, January). *Educational testing in America: What's right, what's wrong?* Keynote presentation at the Third Annual International Conference on Restructuring Curriculum-Assessment-Teaching for the 21st Century, National School Conference Institute, Phoenix, AZ.

Reich, R. B. (1992). *The work of nations.* New York: Vintage.

SCANS. (1991). *What work requires of schools: A SCANS report for America 2000.* Washington, DC: U.S. Department of Labor, Secretary's Commission on Achieving Necessary Skills.

Senge, P. M. (1990). *The fifth discipline.* New York: Doubleday.

Showalter, V., Cox, D., Holobinko, P., Thomson, B., & Oriedo, M. (1974). What is unified science education? *Prism II, 2*(3). (Newsletter, Center for Unified Science Education, Columbus, OH)

Spady, W. G. (1991). Summer implementation seminar: High Success Program on Outcome-Based Education, Seattle, WA.

Taba, H. (1966). *Teaching strategies and cognitive functioning in elementary school children* (Cooperative research project). Washington, DC: Office of Education, U.S. Department of Health, Education, and Welfare; San Francisco: San Francisco State College.

Thurow, L. (1993). *Head to head: The coming economic battle among Japan, Europe, and America.* New York: Warner.

Valencia, S. W. (1991). Portfolios: Panacea or Pandora's box? In F. L. Finch (Ed.), *Educational performance assessment* (pp. 33-46). Chicago: Riverside.

Wang, M. C., Haertel, G. D., & Walberg, H. J. (1993). Toward a knowledge base for school learning. *Review of Educational Research, 63*(3), 249-294.

Index

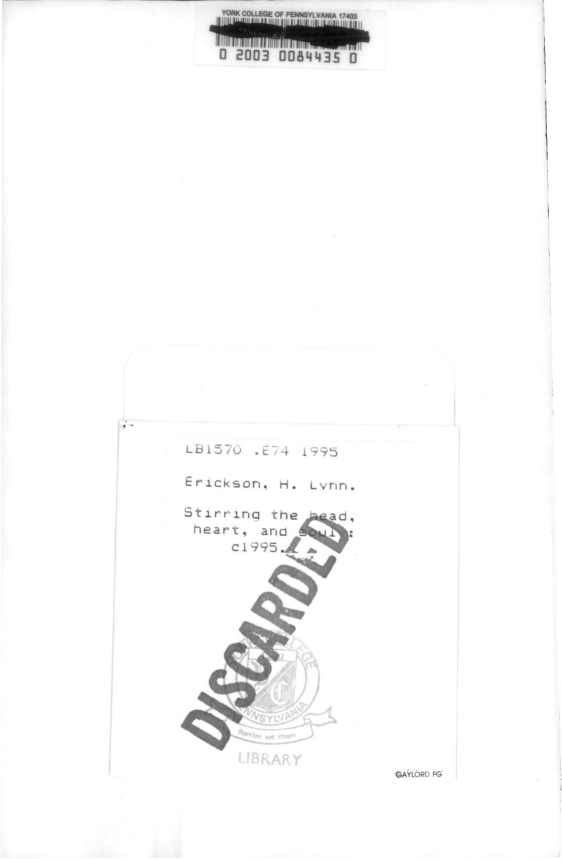